# THE
# PUR**S**UIT

## A GUIDE TO INTERCESSION

Thank you for your purchase!
As you journey through these
pages, may new wells of
faith spring up in you!
— Broderick L. McBride

# THE
# PURSUIT

## A GUIDE TO INTERCESSION

## BRODERICK L. MCBRIDE

### FOREWORD BY LABRYANT FRIEND

Printed in the United States of America

Keen Vision Publishing, LLC

www.publishwithKVP.com

ISBN: 978-1-948270-85-4

*Dedicated to Sandra McBride-Jordan for giving me the gift of prayer, to Tracy Adams for giving me the gift persistence, and to Dorretta Adams for showing me the power of intercession and faith.*

*To those who are committed to the imperfect journey of faith...keep going!*

# CONTENTS

# FOREWORD

The gift and call to the position of an Intercessor is one that many have cast off in hopes and aspirations of being "seen" in ministry. Yet deep in the heart of our families, our local churches, our nation, and even the globe lies the desperate need for men and women who have a reignited passion for the authority of intercession. While we have developed practical applications to almost every part of our faith, one missing element has stemmed around the need to empower and activate the heart of Intercessors. So, while there may be a remnant of individuals that take on the real role and responsibility of Intercessor, authentic material to help cultivate their heart and posture has not always been readily accessible.

It is for times and moments like this that pieces such as The Pursuit become necessary garments that become interwoven in the fabric of the intercessor's life. When we take intercession out of being solely and strictly applicable from a spiritual perspective and begin walking out the delicate nuances of daily carrying these matters out, it takes on a texture and tone in our personal lives that gives us the wherewithal to see every matter from heaven's perspective. This, in turn, develops into intimate moments where the intercessor develops the ear to hear God for themselves, the weapons that are at their disposal, and the wisdom of navigating the art of spiritual warfare.

Though Broderick McBride is a young man, he has inherited the wisdom from men and women of prayer that far exceed his age or maturation as an intercessor. One of the powerful elements that unfolds between the pages of this book is a weight and authority that are received exempt from a natural educational matriculation. Instead, what you gather and step into are the journeys of individuals who have spent time in His presence and subsequently have articulated principles that any individual can apply in their personal journey with God. While Broderick has written with a depth that carries weight and contemplation, the prayer targets married with the places for a deeper personal dig help to sharpen the sensitivity of every intercessor while simultaneously helping them to arrive at their own personal identity as one called to pray.

It is rare to find the passion with competence that you are about to receive through the impartation of this prophetic manual. I believe that every #McBrideMoment and intercessor's tool that will be imparted to you through this read will become tools in your personal intercessor's wheelhouse. Broderick is indeed a man of intercession, and this guide will help you walk through many milestones of his own personal journey that He has watched God heal, restore, and fortify because of his commitment to prayer. This is not just another novel that takes Scriptures to become a glorified sermon in book form. This is the beginning of what I believe will be the blueprint for raising intercessors in places of worship around the globe. Welcome to The Pursuit...

LaBryant Friend
Author, *The Burden of a Builder*

# INTRODUCTION

Authentic prayer should not be used as a mechanism to control other people nor bend outcomes for our selfish pleasures. Instead, prayer is one of the greatest investments of Heaven to Earth, that extends the invitation for supernatural interventions in natural realties. In the Gospels, Disciples made one simple yet profound request of Jesus, "Master, teach us to pray." Jesus' response was giving them a strategy laced in the language of prayer. Even today, the hearts of Believers in Christ are longing to be those, astute in the area of prayer. Prayer is for the risk taker; it is the act of communicating with an entity that we cannot readily interpret with our physical senses. It requires us to move blindly, oftentimes resting in what we perceived to be true with little evidence. It is fueled by our faith, anchored in our God-given identity, stirred by reality, and awaits humanity's engagement. Simply put...creation cannot survive without prayer.

The Pursuit is a book that takes its readers on a journey through prayer. In this book you will examine the identity of the Believer, how to hear the voice of God, the many types of prayer, how to navigate through spiritual droughts, the various tools of the Intercessor, the faith praxis of fasting, and the power of community. This book exists to give language to those who feel disoriented engaging in prayer, and to ignite fires of faith in the hearts of Intercessors.

The halls of history are marked with those who reverently sought-after God and depended on God's power to manifest in Earth's affairs. Martin Luther King Jr, Harriet Tubman, the Moravians, Booker T. Washington, Joan of Arc, Fanny Crosby, George Washington Carver, Dietrich Bonhoeffer, Amy Carmichael, John Brown (the Abolitionist), Nelson Mandela, Madam CJ Walker, Susan B. Anthony, Johannes Kepler, Charles R. Drew, Rebecca Lee Crumpler, the Desert Fathers and Mothers were all people who believed in God and committed themselves to prayer.

Although they were all quite flawed, their humanity could not overshadow their urgency to see God revealed in specific areas of interest. Some of these individuals have documented how their inventions, social justice causes, progressions in medicine, even their influences all exist as a divine response to them venturesomely praying. From science to law, from education to religion, from commerce to war there are men and women who simply believed God for answers. It is true *past, present and future belong to the Intercessor.* The book of Romans insists that all of creation is awaiting the moment the Sons of God would arise. The only way our World will change is if Men as well as Women would pray audacious prayers and tenaciously move in faith.

This book is a treasure trove that should be read over and over again with keen attention to details. Write in the margins, pose questions, research topics in-depth, but most of all be encouraged to pray. The destruction of a nuclear warhead or any type of tyranny is child's play compared to *unprayed* prayers. We should not permit prayerlessness to become the language of our *waiting on* God. It is our responsibility to have faith and pray. It is God's responsibility to manifest God's sovereignty. Welcome to *The Pursuit*.

# MODULE ONE

# HEARING THE VOICE OF GOD

part one

- The Heart of the Intercessor
- Identity: What is Heaven Saying about You?
- Heart Posture Matters
- Four Tools for Navigating through God's Silence

## PRAYER TARGET Your Heart

Ask God to reveal to you what is in your heart and how does God feel about your heart, its disposition, posture, desires, and current state. Specifically ask God how He feels about how you take care of your heart.

## #MCBRIDEMOMENT

Oftentimes the Intercessor can become so consumed in praying for other things we neglect our own lives. Even just doing life as a Human or a Believer can become taxing on our mental capacity to intentionally not place our relationship with God on the "back burner." Taking time to ask God, how God feels about Your heart is an act of maturity and love. Ezekiel 36:26 (AMP) "Moreover, I will give you a new heart and put a new spirit within you, and I will remove the heart of stone from your flesh and give you a heart of flesh."

As Intercessors, one must understand that the lens through which we hear the voice of God is persuaded by two major factors.

- The **first** is our personal view of who the Lord is to us. *How do you see God for yourself? Who is God to you?*
- The **second** is our own individualized life experiences (lived narratives) which include the good, the bad, and the ugly.

*Adam and Eve hid themselves from the voice and presence of God, when they had been VERY familiar with the voice and presence of God.*

Genesis 3:8-10

What happened after being familiar with the voice of God that caused them to run from God's presence after their supposed fall? The act of eating the fruit created a negative persona that was not a part of God's original intent for Adam and Eve. An encounter with a persuasive serpent erected a toxic mental paradigm that affected how they viewed God, themselves, and each other. The new paradigm and persona of this couple, in the Garden of Eden, was developed outside the scope of WHO God envisioned, commissioned, and created them to be (Genesis 1:26-30 & Genesis 2:15-25 NRSV).

A major note for all Intercessors is not just how we see God, but inversely the knowledge of how God sees us. If we healthily know how God views us, we will become instruments of God's demonstration in the Earth. Intercessors with broken lenses are ill-equipped to freely move in their assignment because, again, to hear God clearly, one must know who God is and what God's voice sounds like. To assist Believers and especially the Intercessor with realigning their view of who God is, God uses the Word to build up the identity of His sons and daughters (the Intercessors). Holy Spirit is the greatest catalyst in giving all humanity the language, behavior, and paradigms that are specifically focused on our original, God-given design. Holy Spirit is the full totality of God's mind made accessible to humanity and all creation. Yes, Holy Spirit is a person with emotions, actions, and even employment but, too, Holy Spirit is the fullness of God's intelligence. From this place of being God's intelligence, Holy Spirit informs all creation of who we are, our purposes, but also our identities. We also gain "identifiers" from our environments, relationships (intrapersonal or interpersonal), behaviors, assumptions, and influences.

Depending on the individual, the power of "identifiers" can push us deeper into whom God has commissioned us to be or they can actually cause us to deviate, committing to living below what God has designed us to authentically be. For an example, we have the scriptural promise that God has given us power (might, strength, capacity, or means) to gain wealth [Deuteronomy 8:18]. However, if my environment has been nothing but poverty, surrounded by a people who have been stripped of their capacity to dream, it is quite possible that I, too, may forfeit my ability to gain wealth simply because poverty is all I have even known. Many have become slaves to toxic identifiers simply because of ignorance (Hosea 4:6) and not asking the right questions.

## INTERCESSOR IDENTITY NOTES

Ask yourself: *"Am I a slave or am I a son?"* Many of us approach the office of faith from the perspective that we have no control over ourselves, as if, once we come into the belief of Christ, our lives become robotic, being lulled by the power of God. This is absolutely erroneous! God has still given humanity freewill to willingly pursue God or do as we desire. Many also take this same ideology, of being under the control or power of another entity as an excuse to not break toxic behavior: "I can't help it, I'm a liar…when I want to tell the full truth…I lie. Lying is controlling me and destroying my life." However, nothing can fully control us without our complete yielding (forcible or persuasive) and willful participation.

Asking an identity-based question helps to bring light on where we gather the proof of who we are. Does this intel come from God or from personal venomous views of self? For the intercessor, identity can be defined by answering the question, "HOW does God view me?" vs "HOW I view myself?" Prayer and intercession are engaged from the place of identity.

A Slave is:

- **Forced** to obey
- Someone who is **stripped** of their right to personage
- **Not human** but **legal** property fit to be sold at the owner's will.

When I view myself as a slave, I beg for things that are simply given. I wrestle and fight for things that are solely to be received. I believe that I am unworthy and undeserving of God's best. This lens makes the gift of salvation and the liberty found in Christ Jesus abstract constructs that are impossible to reach. It is a nagging tormentor that attempts to keep humanity from viewing itself the way God sees us. It is my belief that, continuously, Heaven is declaring over humanity who God says we are. *What are the identity lenses Heaven gave you? What specifically has Heaven said about You?*

Here are a few reminders of how God views you:

- **FRIEND** John 15:12-17 (NRSV)

  *"No longer do I call you slaves, for the slave does not know what his master is doing; but I have called you friends, for all things that I have heard from My Father I have made known to you."* (v. 15)

- **MASTERPIECE** Ephesians 2:10 (AMP)

  *"For we are His workmanship [His own master work, a work of art], created in Christ Jesus [reborn from above —spiritually transformed, renewed, ready to be used] for good works, which God prepared [for us] beforehand [taking paths which He set], so that we would walk in them [living the good life which He prearranged and made ready for us]."*

- **SON AND DAUGHTER** 2 Corinthians 6:18

  "And *I will be Father to you, And you will be my Sons and Daughters, says the Almighty God." [ref: Romans 8:15]*

- **HEIR** Romans 8:17 (AMP)

  *"And if [we are His] children, [then we are His] heirs also: heirs of God and fellow heirs with Christ [sharing His spiritual blessing and inheritance], if indeed we share in His suffering so that we may also share in His glory. [ref: Romans 8:15-17 MSG]*

- **TREASURE** Deuteronomy 7:6 (NLT)

  *"For you are a holy people, who belong to the Lord your God. Of all the people on earth, the Lord your God has chosen you to be his own special treasure."*

- **BELOVED** Song of Solomon 2:16 (KJV)

  *"My beloved is mine and I am His..."*

Our understanding of our God-given identity, the inner knowing of who we are to God, is the foundation of our journey as Intercessors. When we authentically understand our significance, we get in touch with the purpose and greatness for which we were created. When we accept this perspective, seemingly challenging life problems become stepping-stones to God-influenced greatness, instead of stumbling blocks of failure. Identity shifts perspectives, and the right perspective enables us to tread across difficulties to our destinies instead of allowing them [difficulties] to stop us in our tracks.

## INTERCESSOR HEART NOTES

The posture of your heart matters. Ask yourself:
- Where is my heart postured?
- What exactly is eating and/or feeding me?
- What is up with these emotions?

Intercessor, remember the Key to Intercession is the <u>POSTURE OF ONE'S Heart!</u> We are the mouthpiece of God, assigned to call the Kingdom of God forth and to also alter history. We can do neither with an ill heart, a preoccupied heart, a sick heart, a hard heart, a bound heart, and etc. Matthew 12:34-36 (MSG) says, "Out of the abundance of the heart the mouth speaks." (v. 34) Now, let's perform some heart surgery.

1. Be vigilant of your heart...it is YOUR responsibility, NOT God's! *See Proverbs 4:23.*
   - Heart is defined as inner man, mind, will, understanding, moral character, the seat of appetites, emotions,

passions, & courage.

2. Toxicity in the heart causes illness in the body! *See Proverbs 14:30 & Proverbs 17:22.*

   • The soundness of our heart can be the health, cure, or remedy our body needs. However, a mispositioned heart that is set in bitterness, rage, grief, restlessness... can dissolve its owner of life [physically, mentally, spiritually].

3. Heart posture reflects the essence of the person! *See Proverbs 15:13 & Proverbs 27:19.*

   • The heart is a mirror, what is displayed from a person is often what is in their hearts.

4. Hard hearts inherit calamity and are robbed of Peace. *See Proverbs 28:14 & Matthew 11:29.*

   • Hearts that are harsh or difficult dethrones peace in the person but also their environment.

5. A bad heart cannot work in faith! *See Matthew 9:21-22 & Mark 11:22-25.*

   • Displaced hearts are disjointed from the gift of faith, and without faith there are no miracles.

6. Hard hearts block understanding and healing. *See Matthew 13:15.*

   • Displaced hearts inhibit our ability to understand and see things clearly.

7. Permit God daily to create your heart. *See Matthew 15:18-19, Jeremiah 17:9 & Psalms 51:10.*

   • Daily we should permit God access to our hearts to manifest God's desire there. To know the quality of a heart, including your own, listen to the words that are spoken. The heart is described as deceitful, fraudulent, polluted and crooked...but it is also defined as a defensive hill [Hebrew word: `aqob] "keeping back those who go up". The heart will fight whoever you give access to it...including God.

8. Intercessor, YOU HAVE TO FORGIVE. See Matthew 18:20-36.

- We must be MASTERS OF FORGIVENESS! Often, we have to 'forfeit our Rights to be right. We can have fully validated, justified rights to feel what we feel. However, for the sake of hearing God clearly and praying prayers that are God-centered, we must become MASTERS OF FORGIVENESS.

Doing the work of healing on the heart is difficult, tiring, gruesome...but WORTH it! We can do it!!! Isaiah 41:10 (AMP)10 "Do not fear [anything], for I am with you; Do not be afraid, for I am your God. I will strengthen you, be assured I will help you; I will certainly take hold of you with My righteous right hand (a hand of justice, of power, of victory, of salvation)". Know that a broken, ill, unforgiving heart is a tool used by the enemy to keep us locked out of destiny and silent! A broken heart cannot hold the promises of God. An infected or sick heart cannot perceive the promises of God!

**The Intercessor MUST master the Art of Forgiveness! The speed of our forgiveness reveals the health of our hearts. THIS IS IMPORTANT because our heart is the Dwelling Place of Faith!**

*"Trust God, when You cannot trace God."*

There WILL be MOMENTS/Seasons where it will feel as if God has gone silent. This is NOT a time to retreat, pout, or throw a temper tantrum!! THIS is actually an opportunity to:

- Remind God of God's word. *Isaiah 43:26, "Put me in remembrance, let us plead together. State your case, that you may be acquitted."*

- Don't forget past God-given victories. *Romans 8:28, "And we know [with great confidence] that God [who is deeply concerned about us] causes all things to work together [as a plan] for good for those who love God, to those who are called according to His plan and purpose."* (How did Paul know this? Reference Acts 27-28, Acts 16:16-40 & Acts 9. Paul survives all of these things prior to writing Romans 8. NEVER forget what YOU survived.)

- Groan, Cry aloud, STAY in the face of God. *See Exodus 2:23-25, Romans 8:26, Psalms 34:17, Psalms 16:11 & Psalm 91:1.*

- Utilize FAITH. *See Hebrews 11:1, Romans 1:17 & Hebrews 11:6.*

# CELEBRATION ASSIGNMENT

### "Dear God"

Write a letter to God, identifying the experiences that have shaped and are currently shaping how you view God. Permit yourself to be vulnerable, HONEST and transparent...this is your space to get 'it' out, forgiving God, <u>YOURSELF</u>, 'them' and 'it' (some of us need to forgive entire cities or even specific decades).

*Additional Note: Get a journal dedicated for the sole purpose of prayer.*

# NOTES

_____

_____

_____

_____

_____

_____

_____

_____

_____

_____

_____

_____

_____

_____

_____

_____

_____

_____

_____

_____

_____

_____

_____

_____

# MODULE TWO

# HEARING THE VOICE OF GOD

## part two

- The Senses, The Word, & Holy Spirit
- Who is the Holy Spirit?

## PRAYER TARGET

Holy Spirit, speak to us, about us. Reveal where we have run and are running from You. Sharpen our ears so that we may hear from You, trust us to be in Your secret counsel again. Equip us to righteously manage Your heart, for the sake of Your Kingdom advancing.

**Amos 3:7** "Surely the Lord God will do nothing without revealing His secret to His servants the prophets."

## #MCBRIDEMOMENT

Many of us struggle with our capacity to "hear" God because we have placed the voice of God into a box. God can get messages to us a number of ways, but God specifically uses our 5-senses to illuminate and download intel to us. God is always speaking but we are not always tuned in to the frequency of God's voice.

# SENSORY NOTE OF INTERCESSION

The revelatory insight to hearing the Voice of God is understanding that there are anatomical expressions that bear witness to the tangible act of 'Hearing God'. We can hear, feel, see, know, and even smell the activity of heaven, concerning humanity, at any given moment. Our function and flow are predicated on how <u>open</u> we are & our <u>level of maturity</u> in spiritual matters.

<u>Audible Voice – Ear</u>

This speaks to our ability to authentically hear the voice of God. The first person to ever encounter the voice of God, from a biblical perspective, is recorded to have been Adam in the garden of Eden. It was the voice of the Lord that gave direction, clarity, defense, correction, purpose, and identity. For humanity, the voice of the Lord does the exact same thing when permitted to do so.

The key to hearing the voice of the Lord is to literally give God's voice intentional audience. God is only heard where we permit God to be heard. We all have the capacity to hear God, but some of us willingly deny God's voice access into our reality; and we have the human right to do so. The second key to hearing the voice of God is consistency! While in the Garden of Eden, Adam had consistency in his engagement with God. It was from his place of consistency that God could trust him to name all things in the garden, that he could rightfully identify things he had never seen, and that he knew who he was. One thing that we can learn from Adam's narrative with the voice of God is: "where there is no consistency there is no strong accuracy of hearing." What we give ear to, gears [adjust or adapt something to suit a special purpose or need] us. Consider the following examples:

- Jeremiah - Jeremiah 1:4-10
- Children of Israel at Mt. Horeb - Deuteronomy 4:9-14
- Samuel - 1 Samuel 3

Sensory – Feel

This pertains to an inner awareness of a thing. In the book of Acts, it is shared that Apostle Paul and Timothy were forbidden by the Spirit of Jesus to enter into a specific place in Asia, to preach the Gospel. This appears to be a conundrum, especially since Christ commissioned the preaching of the Gospel to all Creation [Mark 16:15]. How did Paul and Timothy know that they were not permitted to go into this area to release the good news of Christ? I personally believe they felt the forbidding [hinder, keep from, withstand, not suffer to do] of the Lord. As Believers, many of us can feel the happenings of the Spirit and can explain in detail what we feel with precision. This tool is highly effective in those who intentionally do the inner healing work of keeping themselves clear emotionally. This means being committed to forfeiting the Right to be right!

- Paul & Timothy forbidden - Acts 16:6-7 (AMP)
- Holy Spirit in our conscience mind:
  Romans 9:1 "I am telling the truth in Christ, I am not lying, my conscience testifies with me [enlightened and prompted] by the Holy Spirit."

  Romans 8:16 "The Spirit itself bears witness with our spirit, that we are the children of God."

Holy Spirit at work within the conscience enables us to be God's Co-laborers in the Earth.

# INTERCESSOR IDENTITY NOTES

The Conscience is the place from which self-awareness comes. In this level of the mind, we develop competence, order, dutifulness, achievement striving, self-discipline and deliberation. It contains all thoughts, memories, feelings and wishes that we are aware of at any given moment. This is the part of the mind we can talk about rationally...this part of the brain says, "I care; I consider my impact on others and the World."

## Unction - Inner Knowing:

The unction is nothing more than an inner knowing given by the anointing you carry. Knowing and being aware of something are not the same thing. We can all be aware of the wind blowing, the Sun shining, or even an individual being present in a room but that does not mean we know any of these things. To know something denotes a level of specificity, detail, intimacy and insight.

A solar scientist and a meteorologist have a greater understanding of the Sun and the wind that the average person on Earth will never have. The difference between the scientist and the average person, is their level of commitment to being intimate with the information on a specific subject matter. The unction [GREEK: chrísma] is defined as anointing, anything smeared on, ointment, an unguent used in the inaugural ceremony for priest, kings, and sometimes prophets, any by this they were regarded as endued with the Holy Spirit and divine gifts. Essentially the unction is the anointing of God that brings us into the detailed knowledge...the KNOWING of all things, especially the truth of God.

- Simeon & Anna - Luke 2:25-36

1 John 2:20 (KJV) "But ye have an unction from the Holy One, and ye know all things."

- Paul on the way to Jerusalem - Acts 20:13-38 & Acts 21:1-14

## Visual - Dreams/Visions (Joel 2:28-29)

Dreams are considered to be sleep communication. Since the inception of time and of humanity's ability to sleep, God has used these moments to bring revelatory insight into the Earth. In Old Testament context, a strong indicator of a Prophet was their ability to dream (Deuteronomy 13:1 & Numbers 12:6).

Vision is defined as the state of being able to see, the ability to think about or plan the future with imagination or wisdom. It is my belief that dreams are the byproduct of vision(s). There are two types of visions: open and closed. An open vision is a trance-like state where one receives visual downloads from Holy Spirit while being awake. Open visions come when the conscious mind is being engaged while the person who is seeing the vision is aware. A closed vision is when an individual receives visual downloads from Holy Spirit while asleep. These types of visions are extremely vivid, it is almost as if the individual is opened to another dimension of existence while asleep. Both open and closed visions are accessible to the Believer.

- Abimelech-Genesis 20:3-6
- Joseph-Genesis 37
- Joseph & Magi-Matthew 1:20 & Matthew 2:11-22

## THE WORD [Bible]

It is absolutely useless to have the gifts of God and the capacity to hear God, if there is no discipline to study/read the written word of God. The scripture not only interprets itself, but it also confirms, strengthens, and directs what we perceive from the Holy Spirit via our capacity to see, hear, feel, and know the movements of God. Know that the Word of God will not change, so if you currently cannot discern God, track God via His written word. When God is quiet, know that God's word in the Bible is consistently speaking. Get to reading it!

At the time of writing Daniel 9 (ref. Jeremiah 25:1-11), Daniel had lived in exile for 68 years. He knew they only had 2 years left, but he set his face to pray (Daniel 9:3-4) through the Word of the Lord concerning his people. He did not commit himself to praying from his emotions or even his own human desires, the Prophet's focus was on the promise of God documented in the Book of Jeremiah.

According to Revelation 10:8-11, when John ate the 'scroll' he was given authority/ability to prophesy to people, nations, tongues, and kings. It was his job to prophesy out of the scroll what God had said about these nations. [ref. Revelation 19:10, when we prophesy or pray prophetically, we are not speaking just to the earth realm, we are, in fact, picking up and discerning the present testimony of Jesus in the courts of Heaven.]

## THE BEING OF HOLY SPIRIT

The Holy Spirit is the most 'underemployed' entity in the Triune Godhead. We know God as Father, we understand Jesus to be Savior, Redeemer, Only Begotten Son of God and the Word of God made flesh. However, when it comes to the Being of the Holy Spirit, many of us confine Him to be a 'thing' that causes us to act eccentric/eclectic or as something that cannot quite be explained. In actuality, Holy Spirit is the greatest gift God could have given all Creation access to.

<u>He Has a Mind</u> "And He who searches the hearts knows what the mind of the Spirit is, because the Spirit intercedes [before God] on behalf of [a]God's people in accordance with God's will."(Romans 8:27)

<u>He Has a Will</u> "For those who are living according to the flesh set their minds on the things of the flesh [which gratify the body], but those who are living according to the Spirit, [set their minds on] the things of the Spirit [His will and purpose]."(Romans 8:5)

*"For it seemed good to the Holy Ghost, and to us, to lay upon you no greater burden than these necessary things;"*

Acts 15:28 (KJV)

<u>He Has Emotions</u> "Then I was beside Him, as a master craftsman; And I was daily His delight; Rejoicing before Him always, rejoicing in the world, His inhabited earth, and having my delight in the sons of men."(Proverbs 8:30-31) [ref. Eph. 4:30, Heb. 10:29; Acts 9:31]

<u>He Has a Job/Employment</u> "Now there are [distinctive] varieties of spiritual gifts [special abilities given by the grace and extraordinary power of the Holy Spirit operating in believers], but it is the same Spirit [who grants them and empowers believers]. And there are [distinctive] varieties of ministries and service, but it is the same Lord [who is served]. And there are [distinctive] ways of working [to accomplish things], but it is the same God who produces all things in all believers [inspiring, energizing, and empowering them]. (1 Corinthians 12:4-6)

# CELEBRATION ASSIGNMENT

## "What is stopping me?"

1. Identify the hindrances that keep you out of the presence of God and the things that consume your mind or over prioritize your space.
2. Once you have identified those areas, employ Holy Spirit to grant you wisdom on how to properly handle and disengage them from your life.

*Additional Note: Be honest, be transparent, and look deep. You cannot be free from what you refuse to identify. Call it out and disengage!*

# NOTES

# MODULE THREE

# HEARING THE VOICE OF GOD
part three

- The Soul
- Imago Dei — Without it, there is Hell
- Creativity is the Home of the Miraculous
- How does the Intercessor manifest Creativity?
- What Hearing the Voice of God gives us?
- Why don't we see Manifestations?
- Prayer Rules

## PRAYER TARGET

For the next 7 days pray for an individual using the prayer model of Matthew 6:9-14, for 30 minutes every day.

## #MCBRIDEMOMENT

Throughout the synoptic Gospels there is only one thing the disciples specifically asked Jesus to teach them. According to Luke 11, Jesus' disciples asked Him to teach them to pray, just as John the Baptist had taught his disciples. Prayer is the greatest tool and technology, invested into humanity, that Heaven has given us. Where there is no prayer, there is no Spirit of Christ, and where there is no Spirit of Christ, there is no life. The absence of life is the lack of Creativity, where there is no Creativity...there is hell.

In Genesis 1 & 2, we are introduced to God the Creator who breathed into humanity, causing dust formed bodies to become 'living souls' (Gen 2:7). Genesis 1:26-28 specifically teaches us that humanity is not only created in the IMAGE of God but the LIKENESS [creativity, intelligence, and ingenuity]. Then, in Genesis 2:19-20 Adam was equipped with the capacity to name and properly identify things that he had never seen. In three Old Testament text, we are introduced to some very descriptive themes on the image of God, as it relates to humanity:

- **Genesis 1:26-27 (CEB)** "Then God said, "Let us make humanity in our image to resemble us so that they may take charge of the fish of the sea, the birds in the sky, the livestock, all the earth, and all the crawling things on earth." God created humanity in God's own image, in the divine image God created them, male and female God created them." [the **Final Creative act of the 6th day of Creation**]

- **Genesis 5:1-2 (NASB)** "This is the book of the generations of Adam. In the day when God created man, He made him in the likeness of God. 2 He created them male and female, and He blessed them and named them Man in the day when they were created" [the **Genealogy of Adam to Abraham**]

- **Genesis 9:6 (CEB)** "Whoever sheds human blood, by a human his blood will be shed for in the divine image God made human beings." [**After Noah's Flood, God's Blessing**]

In these three texts the word "image" translates the Hebrew word *selem;* and the "likeness" translates the Hebrew *demût.* The state and the quality of our being/bodies were created on the premise of *Divine Intentionality*...God meant to create humanity this way. Genesis 1 introduces its readers to the notion that the physical appearance of humanity reflects that of the Creator; therefore, physical appearance MUST BE DIVINE!

> *"The marvel of man's bodily appearance is not at all to be excepted from the realm of God's image. This was the original notion, and we have no reason to suppose that it completely gave way to a spiritualizing and intellectualizing tendency. Therefore, one will do well to split the physical from the spiritual as little as possible: the whole man is created in God's image."*[1]
>
> -Gerhard von Rad
> *Genesis: A Commentary, translated by John H. Marks, The Old Testament Library (Philadelphia: The Westminster Press, 1961), p. 56.*

Out of all things created, only Humanity was given dominion over the whole world, this rulership too reflects the very essence of the image we were created in. The Divine Likeness is a relational entity because it is manifested in humanities ability, as well as office, to rule the rest of creation or to coexist exercising dominion and lordship.

## WHY IS THIS IMPORTANT TO THE INTERCESSOR?

The Imago Dei is the expression of God's Spirit in the Earth. Wherever there is human existence there is also the presence of God, because we all carry the Image of God, according to Genesis 1 & 2. _When humanity permits the breaking of relationship, isolation, and even the man issued destruction of life; not only are those works demonic in nature, as well_ _as sinful, but they are also full manifestations of Hell._ Hell is nothing more than the absence of the Presence and Spirit of God, and where there is no God there is no creativity!

Creation's introduction to God is solely as Creator, it is the original context by which all things that exist (even down to the molecular level) experienced God. It is from this initial place, God formed bodies for all things living and by using the technology of breath, humanity receives the gift of _soul_ (the seat of our will, intentions, intellect, emotions and decision making).

This 'gift' gave humanity the capacity to function in a way that no other created entity can. The natural human ability to engage creativeness reflects our connectivity and communion with God, the Creator (**which is why devotional life is of absolute importance**). Creativeness manifests and dispenses Heaven on Earth and it is responsible for the advancement of God's kingdom on Earth. **CREATIVITY is the home and origin for <u>miracles, signs and wonders, and is the place of solution.</u>**

## HOW DO WE MANIFEST CREATIVITY EXPRESSED IN OUR DIVINE NATURE?

1.  **Praise** is a technology and concept that is expressed through the instrument of creativity. It is an act of intentionality, passion, and love. It can be spontaneous, calming, and invigorating. Praise can literally be all things and nothing at the same time, however the consistent variable in praise is its direction. Praise should always be focused upon past, present, and future manifestations of who God is. Here are some expressions of Praise:

    *   **Barak** to kneel in humility, to bless, to salute a King (Genesis 1:22, Genesis 5:2, Psalm 115:18, 2 Chronicles

6:13, 2 Samuel 8:10)

- **Halal** to praise, celebrate, sing praises and boast about with shouting and jubilation (2 Samuel 6:14-16)
    - Songs, hymns, spiritual songs (Ephesians 5:17-20)
- **Shabach** to address in a loud tone, to commend, to stroke, still or soothe (Psalm 63:3, Psalm 65:7)
- **Tehillah** Singing focusing on deeds and qualities worthy of praise, praise that is demanded based off deeds and/or attributes (Exodus 15:11, Deuteronomy 10:21)
- **Towdah** extending of the hand, the offering of sacrificial praise, thanksgiving in liturgical worship (Jonah 2:9, Amos 4:5, Isaiah 51:3)
- **Yadah** wringing of hands in praise, to throw or cast hands in praise, to confess the name of God and/or sins (2 Chronicles 7:6, 2 Chronicles 6:26, 2 Chronicles, Leviticus 5:5)
- **Zamar** playing instruments (Psalm 33:2, Psalm 71:22)

Praise originates from a place of humility and reverence; I cannot praise what I do not deem worthy of adoration (**barak**). In the posture of thanksgiving, praise identifies God's character and bears witness to God's mighty acts that are both seen and unknown (**towdah and yadah**).

Praise is cyclical in that it declares to both Creation and Creator (all things that were created when God said, "Let there be" and to the God who said, "Let there be") God's reputation, magnificence and notoriety (**tehillah**). It is oftentimes uncontainable, flamboyant, celebrative (**halal and shabach**). However, it is sometimes voiced in melodious expressions, including both singing and music (**zamar**) that can be used as an expression of war, fanfare, love and announcement. Essentially praise can be defined as an act of admiration, applause and amplifying God from a heart posture of thanksgiving, for His character, fame, glory, acts, and divine deity—that is directed to God or indirectly others—via words, embodiment, musical instruments, singing and other celebratory actions.

In **2 Chronicles 20:20-24,** King Jehoshaphat uses the military tactic of Shock and Awe with praise literally leading the way. The kingdom of darkness torments the creatives and solutionist heavily because what they produce brings absolute answers that stop systemic cycles of oppression. For this reason, Hell contends against praise, and humanity contends for praise. Wherever there is no praise, there is no habitation of God; and where God does not dwell, THERE is Hell (Psalms 22:3)

2. **Worship** is the act of declaring the Name of God and identifying who God has revealed God's self to be in our personal narrative. It is the act of calling God by name, pulling on personal history with God, and from that place releasing love onto God but also declaring the reality that we will see God in ways far greater than what we have experienced. (Hebrews 13:15 & Psalm 91:15) Worship gives us a greater scope of God, both past present and future in a moment of engagement.

3. Wherever there is the act of **INTIMACY** something will be created. Intimacy is intentional, it is the expression of being fully seen, felt, heard, and accepted with no strings attached. When we engage with being intimate with God, via our devotional lives, we set the stage for

God to move in the Earth through us. It is impossible for the Believer to reign in the Earth as God's representative, if we have not spent time with the Originator of the image [Hebrew word: *selem*] that we reflect.

Praise, Worship, and Intimacy gives humanity the divine connection to authentically hear the voice of the Lord. When we hear God, we are illuminated, enlightened and stripped of the excuse of not knowing *how, what, where, when, or why.* Hearing God's voice kills indecisiveness in the mature and builds fervor to grow in the immature.

## WHAT HEARING THE VOICE OF GOD GIVES US?

1. Life Fulfillment/Identity
   - Genesis 32:24-32 - The fight for life fulfillment and securing identity in God, is found in our relentless contending for what has been rightly promised to us. We receive the ability to wrestle when we have heard the voice of the Lord on the matter. Although Jacob took Esau's birthright and blessing, he was still earmarked by Heaven to be the one through whom Earth's Redeemer would come and all the nations would be blessed (ref. Genesis 27:34-38), through the conception of Judah and the lineage of King David we get Jesus. But before Jesus, we have a Trickster that wrestled for what was promised before he was conceived (Genesis 17, God's Promise to Abraham, Jacob's Grandfather). The voice of God is the instrument used to give humanity the Word of God. Where there is word, there is revelation.

2. Faith

- Romans 10:17 - *"So faith comes from hearing [what is told], and what is heard comes by the [preaching of the] message concerning Christ."* The origin of faith is found in what we have heard [the voice of God and the Word of God]. Our ability to live and be the Source of God's personal pleasure is found in our Faith (ref. Habakkuk 2:4b & Hebrews 11:6). All of creation lives in the dichotomy of *Facts vs Truth.* Facts are based on circumstantial information that is dependent upon external factors that are constantly changing (people, places, things, time, etc). Fact is, you are currently reading this manual. This *fact* will no longer exist once you have moved on to something else. Truths are absolute, they are never changing. I define truth as being the Word of God. Facts may suggest a grim diagnosis, but Truth declares healing *by the shed blood of Jesus Christ* (Isaiah 53:5). We change the outcome of facts with *truths.*

3. Intel

- God does nothing in the Earth without revealing it to the Prophets. **Amos 3:7** "Surely the Lord God does nothing, unless He reveals His secret to His servants the prophets." If we intentionally spend time talking to God and let God speak to us, we will be properly equipped to ask and WILL receive. God gives information to the Believer as a form of strategy, to ensure our movements are consistently productive. It is my belief that when there are moments of emergency in the life of a

Believer, sometimes the root cause can be found in prayerlessness.

We dissolve the panic of emergency by our commitment to 'daily prayer'. Daily prayer eliminates/solves the problem of emergency. It grants us the resources to cover *emergency petitions* because we have spent time in the presence of God. So, when life presents "emergencies" and/or difficult life moments we are not readily moved because our 'time spent' in God's presence *has prepared us for* what *facts* are presented.

Spend time in prayer, then go back and study the Word of God, and God Himself will begin to speak to you! God refuses to cover the emergencies of those that do not talk to Him. Where there is no intimacy, there is no obligation. Giving God preference over your time is an act of faith that moves Heaven. Our time spent with God should not be laced with vain begging and repetitions regarding our own lives. Jesus admonishes us to "seek first the kingdom of God and His righteousness and all things will be added unto you." (**Matthew 6:25-34**). Master the ART of PRAYING FOR OTHERS, then whatever you need... before you request, will be added to you.

## WHY DON'T WE SEE MANIFESTATION?

1. **Prayer Rules-** Rules are defined as *a set of explicit or understood regulations or principles governing conduct within a particular activity or sphere.* This is also known as *metron, the sphere of influence and authority.* I believe prayer is an environment and system that has regulations which affects accuracy & potency of the Intercessor.

2. **Prayer Jurisdiction-** Jurisdiction is defined *as the official*

*power to make legal decisions and judgments.* Could it be that many of us don't see manifestations in prayer because we are asking for and pursuing things that are beyond our 'metron', as well as outside our measure of faith? (**Romans 12:3**) Never ask Heaven for something your faith is not mature enough to grasp or maintain. Essentially, this is the Intercessor's delegating and decision-making authority. There is no ground for double mindedness, ego, or fear here.

3. **Prayer Government-** Government is defined as *the relationship between the governing body and the governing word.* As an Intercessor, our access to the government of Heaven shows up in whatever environment we are in simply because we are a *governing body.* We are all ambassadors of Heaven due to the indwelling of Holy Spirit, and as ambassadors we represent the government from which we came: Heaven (**Philippians 3:20**). The *governing word* is the Word of God, it is the 'legal document' that sustains us. We are ineffective, as a *governing body*, when we lack in-depth awareness and sole reliance on the *governing word.*

According to Luke 11, the only thing the disciples asked Jesus to teach them was simply HOW to pray. I find it interesting that as our world progresses, there is a slow regression from the fundamentals of our Faith. Many of us are more interested in the miraculous, deliverance, and prophecy than we are the simple praxis of prayer. Jesus admonishes the disciples to serve others in prayer (pray for someone else other than yourself), knowing that what they stood in need of is handled. I believe this rings true for the Believer today. When we boldly approach the throne of grace, we should do so from the knowledge of 'what we need, we already have'. Though the facts of life may insinuate something completely opposite, just know YOU HAVE GOD'S PROMISE (1 Corinthians 1:20).

***Remember in Job's story, his predicament did not change until he prayed for his friends Job 42:10***

# RULES OF PRAYER [Matthew 6:9-14, Luke 11:2-5]

1. **"Our Father"** We must understand that God is the MAIN source for the person we are praying for, God is their ultimate source. If we were to bless them as their source, we would mess them, ourselves, and their God-given process up. [Mt 6:9]
   - *"Lord, unveil to them that You alone are their Source."* Pray that their understanding will be opened to KNOW that God is their Source.

2. **"in Heaven"** We must understand that heaven is our home [ref.1 Peter 2:11, Philippians 3:20]
   - *"Lord, make them sensitive to the Spiritual Realm and the matters of Heaven."* Pray that they are made aware that Heaven rules everything of this Earth [Mt 6:9]

3. **"hallowed be thy name"** May God's Character be Revealed to them [Mt 6:9]
   - STUDY the names of God. Ask God to release God's self in YOU and them
   - Pursue to understand God by God's Character and not God's Reputation

4. **"Thy Kingdom Come"** We ask for the purpose of God to be revealed in the lives of His people [Mt 6:10]
   - Pray knowing that each thing God created has a divine purpose that ONLY God can reveal.

- Posture yourself to receive intel; pray with expectation (Amos 3:7)

5. **"Thy Will be done"** We ask that the perfect will of God be performed and carried out in their lives [Mt 6:10]

6. **"Give us this day our daily bread"**- May God sustain them daily with what they need, want and desire [Mt 6:11]

7. **"And forgive us our debts as we forgive our debtors"** God, forgive those who have been wronged and forgive the wrongdoer. [Mt 6:12]
   - Pray for the victim and the victimizer.
   - Ask God to forgive them and that they forgive themselves.

8. **"And lead us"** Ask God to give them guidance [Mt 6:13]
   - Pray that their steps are ordered and led by God

9. **"not into temptation"** May God deliver them from temptation [Mt 6:13]
   - *"God, don't permit them to be in a situation that their flesh will cause them to give in."*
   - NEVER let them be tempted above their power and knowledge

10. **"deliver us from evil"** May God deliver them from demonic assignments that hell has released upon their lives [Mt 6:13]

11. **"thine is the kingdom"** Pray that God manifest **all** the gifts and anointing that He has placed in them [Mt 6:13]

12. **"the power, and the glory"** Pray that God gives them humility, that God keeps them humble.

# CELEBRATION ASSIGNMENT

## "Forfeiting the Right to be Right"

1. For the next 7 days, pray for a person you do not like, strongly disagree with and/or attempt to avoid whenever possible.

   - Pray a minimum of 30 minutes for them per-day
   - Use Matthew 6:9-14 for scriptural base, and the 12 points outlined in "Rules of Prayer."

2. Employ Holy Spirit to intercede through you for the person you have identified.

*Additional Note: Your negative feelings may be totally valid. However, as Intercessors, we never pray from the place of our emotions! We choose to forfeit our Right to be right, so that we be ambassadors of Heaven on the Earth. This ultimately teaches us how to stay focused on the bigger picture.*

# NOTES

_____
_____
_____
_____
_____
_____
_____
_____
_____
_____
_____
_____
_____
_____
_____
_____
_____
_____
_____
_____
_____

# HEARING THE VOICE OF GOD (part three)

# MODULE FOUR

# A CALL TO INTERCESSION

- Intercession vs. Prayer, what is it?
- Jurisdiction of Prayer
- Exousia and Dunamis
- 12 Types of Intercessor

## PRAYER TARGET

Pray that your identity as an Intercessor comes alive with great burden. Specifically pray that your *gift*, calling and mandate for intercession be quickened and brought to life. Employ the Holy Spirit to take you deeper into various functions and areas of intercession.

## #MCBRIDEMOMENT

The lack of proper identity has caused a number of Believers to settle at being novice in the things God has called all of us to. Becoming mature in God begins at identifying where you are and where God has directed you to go. As Intercessors, one of the greatest tools we could ever utilize is being able to discern, identify and function as the Beings God has enabled all of us to be. I believe the door to revelation, and ultimately identity, is information.

**INTERCESSION** I in • ter • se • shun I (verb) 1. To intercede, on the behalf of another and/or to assail or urge anyone with petitions 2. To come between, derived from Latin word intercedo [to obstruct, to interpose on the behalf of a person, place or thing, to intercede] 3. To make intercession and/or to strike upon' or 'against' an opposing force.

**INTERCESSOR** I in • ter • se • sur I (noun) [Hebrew: paga *"paw-gah"*] to impinge, by accident or violence, or by importunity to come betwixt, cause to entreat, to fall (upon), to make intercession, intercessor, intreat, lay, light (upon), meet (together), pray, reach, run.

- **Impinge** Encroach, entrench, advance, move on, take advantage, trespass
- **Importunity** Urgency, coaxing, dunning, insistence, nagging, persistence, pestering, plaguing, plying, pressing
- **Entreat** Beseech, bid, press, plead
- **Intercession** Intervening, engagement, involvement, participating, mediation, petition, prayer

**Intercession** is praying **with God**; it is literally directed from Heaven to Earth and ultimately the act of co-laboring with God. It is the overall act of praying for **people** (individuals and people groups), **places** (cities, states, countries, regions & nations) and **things** (government, systems of this world, spheres of influence), whereas **personal petition** is asking God for daily needs and for God's will to happen in our personal lives.

**Prayer** is directed from Earth to Heaven, it is the act of talking to God about Earth's affairs. Intercession is the act of declaring what God has said about a specific person, place or thing in faith and being tenacious enough to not let up until what God has said is seen in the physical. This is not a passive skill, intercession requires a level of grit, aggression and longevity...it literally requires an activation of the Fruit of the Spirit [Galatians 5:22-23].

The **purpose** of the Intercessor is to be a **mediator** and **build a wall** for those whose lives are being looted and misused. All while remaining covert, as to ensure all glory goes to God. Being a person of prayer is not about being 'seen' or gaining a stage, in the natural, to show how powerful you are; it is not a self-centered/self-serving gift. However, authentic intercession is about living a surrendered life that Christ has the capacity to shine through (Matthew 6:5-6).

The power and authority the Believer has in prayer and intercession is found solely in Jesus Christ and the being of Holy Spirit, dwelling inside of us. I believe that Jesus Christ was the fullness of God wrapped in flesh, meaning Jesus was 100% God and 100%. While on Earth He walked in both POWER (dunamis - miracles) and AUTHORITY (exousia- force, influence). Authority is delegated, released, or given by one who is Superior (Jesus) to one who is Subordinate (the Believer). The Subordinate (the Believer), once given authority, has the ability to function in the same capacity the Superior (Jesus) would in a specific area. Hence, Jesus' reference in Luke 10:19 - through His power and example, the Body of Christ has authority over all the power of the enemy.

Authority can increase or decrease depending on whether a person (the Believer) is in submission to and in proper **knowing** of their relationship with the One Who (Jesus) gave the authority. I have also learned, too, that this authority functions much like a physiological muscle in that the more you use it, the stronger you become, and in the same token the less we use it or abuse it, the more at risk we become at remaining impotent and extremely weakened.

The **Jurisdiction of Intercession** (Prayer Jurisdiction) is directly connected to favor and authority, and those (favor and authority) are rooted in our relationship with the Lord [**SEE Chapter 1 - Intercessor Identity Notes:** *HOW God views me vs HOW I view myself*]. From the posture of "Friend" (See John 15:12-17), we enter into the place of selflessness, trust, intimacy, and endowment. As Friend, we are called to intercession as an act of laying down our lives for others. In this posture, God also makes Himself - His heart - vulnerable to His friends. Intercessors have the phenomenal capacity to manifest as the hands, feet, voice, and body of God at any given moment, but we must remain consistent to living a life of intentional devotion to God.

I believe that there are several functions and types of Intercessors. Some of us can even be hybrid (multitype) Intercessors. Our Intercessor type is subject to change depending on our assignment, maturity, and capacity. Needless to say, the list I provide below is not an exhaustive list. However, I do intend for it to serve as a guide for those who are in beginner stages of Intercession, in dire need of help in identifying language that express their pressures. I also provide *hindrances* that are specific to the Intercessor Types, pay close attention and attempt to avoid them at all cost.

# 12 TYPES OF INTERCESSOR

*Issues Intercessor*

These Individuals are used by God the most during times of 'issues' between groups of people or when an individual is experiencing tough 'life moments' (injustices, addictions, poverty, unfair treatment, demonically-influenced hardships, etc). The Issues Intercessor intercedes for persons, families, circles of influence and nations who cannot stand for themselves. They are deputized by Holy Spirit with burdens of prayer. Some prayer assignments can last for a lifetime. The Issues Intercessor is oftentimes led to pray for individuals they are not too familiar with. God will wake them up very late at night or in the early morning to intercede for a person.

With Holy Spirit as their guide, Issues Intercessors are shown what to pray for but groaning, speaking in tongues and tears are common modes of prayer these intercessory types display. Jesus is the Chief Intercessor (Romans 8:34), but He also functioned as an Issues Intercessor in the life of Peter prior to His crucifixion and Peter's denying betrayal (Luke 22:31-34). Jesus knew what Peter was to become, and how Satan came to steal, kill and destroy that assignment. However, Jesus interceded for him that the assignment of Hell would not be fulfilled in Peter's life. What did that prayer sound like?

## Hindrances for Issues Intercessors

- *Spiritual Gossip:* gaining intel from Holy Spirit about a specific person, place or thing and taking it to other people for the sake of discussing what was revealed. Some intel is meant solely for the one who received it! Before you share anything Holy Spirit has shown you, please go back and get His release before sharing!

- Issues flow out of their own hurts. They tend to pray for issues they readily identify with verses receiving the burden from Holy Spirit

- Misguided passion becoming obsessive and overly courageous with no wisdom

- Not taking time to rest or pause in the presence of God, but continue to move from issue to issue

- Being intolerant of people who seemingly devalue or seem impartial to their "issue" prayer burden. Be mindful that God uses us according to our personality types, there are some things some personality types cannot handle.

- Using your own efforts and soulish love to utilize gifts (false burden). Please assess often where your burden comes from and ask Holy Spirit if your grace for that burden has lifted? If so, be okay with moving on.

*Hinge Intercessor*

Joseph, Esther, Elijah and Abigail (**Genesis 41:46-53, Esther 5:2-8, Esther 7:2-9, 1 Kings 17, 1 Samuel 25:23-33**) all functioned in this specific Intercessor type, they had the power to speak a word, make a request, or even deposit a word that changed the course of history. These individuals literally function like the hinges of a door; they are burdened to open and close portals. They have been positioned by Heaven to affect Earth's history and narrative. Their entire life has been a classroom of sorts, preparing them for the single moment they would be needed most to shift culture, history and world events.

Based on a single word from a Hinge Intercessor, people of great power and influence will make decisions that impact history with undeniable change. The authority of a Hinge Intercessor comes from living a life submitted to God for the development of their character.

These people are highly gifted, and impeccable in character which makes them trustworthy to listen to. *Your gift makes room for you, but your character keeps you in the space open to you because of your gifting* (**Proverbs 18:16**).

## Hindrances for Hinge Intercessors

- Procrastination: a form of idolatry rooted in the belief that you have time to complete a task or you are good enough to fulfill an assignment once you are under pressure. We must solely rely on God to get the job done through us.

- Lack of boldness, fear

- Self-doubt

- Becoming overwhelmed with guilt if they miss an opportunity to intercede

- Looking for or creating a moment or crisis that does not exist for the sake of gaining access to people of influence. This is emotional manipulation and the essence of witchcraft.

*List Intercessor*

The prophet Ezra functioned in this role. He was a priest-scribe that interceded consistently on the behalf of an entire nation. This intercessor type is deemed to be highly dependable and extremely loyal to their prayer assignments. They typically write out everything on a list that they pray over consistently. Oftentimes they spend extensive periods of time in prayer when given a list to focus on. List intercessors have endurance in prayer. They oftentimes will not let up on assignments. Where there is structure, the List Intercessor finds freedom. Order has to be set so that they do not forget prayer targets or focuses.

I believe Jesus, too, functioned as a List Intercessor on the behalf of the nameless woman caught in adultery in John 8. When Jesus began to write on the ground, His writings and words exonerated the woman from the judgment rendered. Authentic intercession overturns the judgment of the enemy and employs mercy. List Intercessors can be found writing prayers out as well, they sometimes purchase journals for the sole use of prayer. Their pen is an instrument of the Lord's warfare!

### Hindrances for List Intercessors

- Can become overwhelmed by the length of their list after a while when they do not have time to cover it all. It is important that the List Intercessor remains mindful of pace and also that all things on their lists are God's responsibility.

- Frustration, especially in corporate settings, when everything on the list is not covered. Corporate settings are often laced with spontaneity and the List Intercessor must remain agile.

- Thinking that using list is the only way to pray, lack of flexibility

- Becoming discouraged when prayers go unanswered, especially when reviewing lists. Be consistently mindful that God is sovereign and cannot be manipulated by our sacrifice, actions, words, or thoughts. God moves when God moves and unanswered prayer could be God's protection wrapped in what we deem to be delay. Steady your heart and know that God heard you the first time you prayed.

*Personal Intercessor*

These are individuals who have a God-given burden to pray for those deemed to be destitute and vagabonds. They may also have a burden to pray for leaders (pastors, missionaries, spiritual leaders, media people, celebrities, businessmen/women, governmental leaders, educational leaders). As personal watchmen, they have been selected by God to intercede for specific individuals and their families.

Holy Spirit strategically grants them access to intel, straight from the Throne Room, regarding what Heaven desires for a person's future, protection, provision, and prayer priorities. With this intel, the Personal Intercessor serves as God's co-laborer in the Earth, agreeing with, praying through and believing in faith for what has been revealed to them. These people carry a **shamar anointing**, they are DEFENDERS, and they are commissioned by heaven to prevent God's people from being deceived or becoming instruments of deception.

Both Apostle Paul (Galatians 3, his words to the churches of Galatia) and Mordecai (Esther 3 & 4, he gathered a nation to intercede and fast on Esther's behalf) served in this role to the lives they were called to serve. In studying their lives, it is readily seen how selfless they were in fulfilling their assignments. Personal Intercessors be mindful that what you are called to do is much bigger than you! They are sometimes employed to an assignment only for a short season. KEEP A JOURNAL for confirmation purposes.

<u>Hindrances for Personal Intercessors</u>

- Seeking the approval of the person they are burdened to pray for. Being a Personal Intercessor to a person does not always equate to being in their direct proximity. The only approval you need is from God.

- Can easily become indifferent to prayer assignments when other people do not validate their burden to pray.

- Selfishness

- Spiritual Gossip in the form of 'bragging' about who they have a burden to pray for and even the sharing of highly confidential intel they have received from Holy Spirit

- Not depending on Holy Spirit for intel on Prayer Assignment

*People Group & Nation Intercessor:*

Very similar to Personal Intercessors, however this Intercessor Type has a God-given burden for entire demographics (people groups), not individuals. These **people groups** can refer to any cluster of populaces based on similar background, socioeconomic status, residence, occupation, health, knowledge, religion, race, or nationality. Holy Spirit grants the Intercessor the gift of mercy, causing them to identify with the people group He has burdened them for. They have a high level of emotional intelligence making them sensitive and aware of the need for reconciliation amongst people groups both internally and externally.

Their prayers are oftentimes salvation-focused, for the gospel to penetrate the masses. They're centered on justice, for God to raise up Deliverers amongst them, and even for Christ to be revealed to them in such a way that the hearts of entire people groups surrender to His wooing. This type of Intercessor may even be led by God to serve as a missionary to specific lands to pray, serve, and live. Moses & Aaron (Numbers 16:35-49), Elijah on Mt. Carmel (1 Kings 18:30-39), and Abraham (Genesis 18) are all examples of People Group Intercessors; they were all individuals who cried out to God for interventions that would turn the hearts of nations to God.

## Hindrances for People Group & Nation Intercessors

- Distraction, birthed out of consistent demonic opposition and heavy warfare, could cause a People Group Intercessor to abort their mission in prayer.

- Discouragement, due to only a small group of people sharing their burden to pray for a specific people group.

- Consistently guard their hearts, because they can develop hatred for the oppressors of the people group, they feel burdened to pray for. Always be mindful that the only enemy we have is the Kingdom of Darkness. We do not fight against other people (Ephesians 6:12)

- Lack of knowledge to God's calendar can lead to being impatient when praying. All things, including the blessings and answers of the Lord, have a *set time, appointed time, and fullness of time.*

*Soul Intercessor*

These persons have a heavy burden for the manifested power of redemption and salvation. They are readily moved by the reality of hell and the consequences of sin for those who are outside the Body of Christ. They are the physical embodiment of 1 Timothy 2:4, earnestly praying that all come into the full knowledge of God's saving grace and the truth of the Holy Spirit. They can be extremely effective praying some of the most unrighteous people and threats into the Kingdom of God. God will oftentimes reveal to them blinders in the lives of their prayer assignment (individual or people group) which will position the Soul Intercessor to pray Heaven's heart concerning the people.

They tenaciously intercede for the backslidden and lost, to the point of anguish, that the soul be saved. There will be moments where the Soul Intercessor will not have words but a travail when praying for a particular soul of an individual or people group. They function heavily in Prophetic, Warfare and Mercy (Deliverance) Intercession. Matching this Intercessor with the preaching of the Gospel or an Evangelist would reap a large harvest of souls: Ananias (Acts 9), Paul praying for regions (Acts 16), City of Nineveh for God's mercy (Jonah 3).

### Hindrances for Soul Intercessors

- Discouragement. Oftentimes Soul Intercessors are not given the opportunity of witnessing the harvest they have been praying for. They could become discouraged because they don't too often receive the praise report about the harvest of souls taking place within a particular people group or region that they have been targeting in prayer.

- Once a soul has been saved, the Soul Intercessor could possibly lack direction on where to go or what to target next.

- Can become overly invested in the spiritual progress of a new convert. Always be mindful of your role, once it has been completed be okay with stepping away so that the next teacher/intercessor can step forward (**1 Corinthians 3:6-9**). We are all on the same team.

- Can permit themselves to suffer in their personal devotional life. Oftentimes we can become burdened with praying for a person, that we forget we were created to commune with God. NEVER PERMIT YOUR PERSONAL RELATIONSHIP WITH GOD TO DIE.

- Succumb to pride because their prayers resulted in a large influx of souls being won for the kingdom

- Can fall prey to condemnation for taking on the personal responsibility of another's right to choose

*Mercy Intercessor*

The Lord usually utilizes this type of Intercessor to release God's heart over a specific people, nation, and/or issue. They are God's stethoscopes, who hear dually the hearts of the hurting (readily identifying trauma) and the Heart of God. Often found weeping, the Mercy Intercessor is used as an instrument to cleanse and soften hardened places in the soul, mind, and realities. They are deeply grieved for the things that break the Heart of God.

These types of intercessors carry a burden for their enemies. There will be times in which they will even weep for their enemies as if they are weeping for their friend. They extend forgiveness rather than judgment, and wherever judgment is imminent, they cry out for the mercy of the Lord to prevail. They understand that **all of humanity** is the Friend of God, even when we operate as the antithesis of that identity, and they tenaciously pray that we come into the full knowledge of that God-given identity. Moses (Numbers 12), Hezekiah (Isaiah 38), and Jeremiah (Jeremiah 4 & 8) are men who wept and prayed for the mercies of God to manifest for a person, a nation, and even themselves.

## Hindrances for Mercy Intercessors

- Ostracized because they utilize the technology of weeping

- Lack resolve with being used in this type of intercession

- Become angry with God when witnessing the suffering of an individual or group

- Fear: may become leery of releasing a word of correction to those for whom they have prayed (Proverbs 27:6)

### Government Intercessors

These individuals are positioned as watchmen over political and church governments that represent various countries, states, cities, neighborhoods, homes, schools and churches. They strongly have faith in the power of intercession to produce change for nations, systems of the world, and the Body of Christ at large. They have the God-given desire to cover their leaders in local, state, and national governments as well as worldwide institutions, depending on the *measure of faith*, focus and discipline they decide to utilize.

Government Intercessors are often supernaturally aware of socio-political issues, legislations, court decisions, elections, and political structures that directly affect entire nations, and they intercede for the intervention of God. They are led to pray "on-site with insight", they are often strategically placed by God behind the scenes, so that they can impact influence. Praying for the government and the Church is one of the greatest privileges that God has given us. [Nathan and Daniel were Court Prophets who also functioned as Governmental Intercessors. Their being in the proper place positioned Heaven's interventions to occur in political structures of their times].

## Hindrances for Government Intercessors

- Self-isolation. They become so concerned with the government that they lose sight on the value of people overall.

- Compromise. Once in places of influence, they compromise personal beliefs and integrity to please people. They can be guilty of people pleasing and even be silent when it is most pressing to speak up.

- They can become intolerant and hostile towards those who appear to be uninformed about the issues of the land.

- Fearful of speaking truth to power, because of possible repercussions.

### Financial Intercessor

The financial intercessors are synchronized with God to call funds in, on the behalf of others and themselves, all for the sake of advancing God's kingdom on Earth. The Financial Intercessor often may not have material resources themselves, but they pray that God prick the hearts of those who do have the gift of giving and/or *helps* (2 Corinthians 9:6-8, 1 Corinthians 12:28).

The amount of finances they have does not matter to them; they are rich in financial miracles, and have faith for the funding of projects and events. God partners with them to protect the finances of others and to also move the hearts of those with the gift of giving.

Financial Intercessors are divinely given insight to financial breakthrough and are taught by Holy Spirit on how to overthrow barriers. They are found praying that funds are used wisely and righteously, and that God exposes anyone that attempts to leech Heaven's earthly resources. They also pray for the protection of other's finances to overcome Satan's attempts to undermine the work of ministry by destroying the financial base from which it is financed. Some are asked to live by faith in their personal lives as a gift of giving is released through them to others; other times God raises up financial intercessors in order to give them supernatural ideas [Joseph was a Financial Intercessor].

## Hindrances for Financial Intercessors

- Bondage to the thought that they have to be lucrative financially to believe God for the financial blessings of others.

- Condemnation and doubt due to seemingly insurmountable personal financial issues

- Overly focused on how God will produce the financial miracle needed. Rest in the fact that God is the 'how'. That is all the information needed to stay focused.

- Belief that righteous acts and good works can manipulate God to bless and send increase, when we receive from God simply because we are God's children (Matthew 7:11).

*Worship Intercessor*

These intercessory types are captivated by the sound, lyric, and instrumentation of Heaven. They find themselves singing songs, releasing chants, hearing chords, etc. during their personal prayer time and may even use song as their entrance into prayer. Worship Intercessors have been divinely appointed by God to even release the songs God is singing over a person or congregation (Zephaniah 3:17 & Psalm 32:7) that translates into tangible comfort, encouragement and strength to the listener.

Because their lyrics come from the Heart of God, they carry breakthroughs that break down walls and ramparts of opposition. Worship intercessors live a life of worship not only by singing but also by word and deeds. They are gifted by God with a desire to Worship Him in spirit and in truth. They walk the fine line between WORSHIP, WARFARE, and INTIMACY [Hannah (Luke 1:46-55) and Jehoshaphat with the Tribe of Judah (2 Chronicles 20) functioned as Worship Intercessors].

**Hindrances for Worship Intercessors**

- Can be easily wounded and take on feelings of rejection when people do not respond well to their worship.

- Focusing more on production and not the authentic presence of God. They can be found putting their gift before God, placing more value on the gift and the instrument and less on the *Manufacturer* of the gift (Romans 11:29)

- Fear. They sometimes resist moving in the anointing God gave them out of fear of comparison, one person to another.

- Perfectionism of voice, lyric, sound and other external factors

- Lack of discipline and agility; sometimes the Holy Spirit may move in a different direction corporately, but the Worship Intercessor wants to stay in a specific flow.

## Warfare Intercessors

They are the physical embodiment of Jehovah Sabaoth's (The Lord of Host, The Lord of Angelic Armies) arsenal in the place of Intercession, fighting and winning victories for the sake of manifesting TRUTH and AUTHORITY, that only comes from Holy Spirit. God uses these Intercessor types to oppose and obliterate Satanic strongholds, while ushering in the liberating truth of God.

A stronghold is a continual and prevalent thought pattern of an individual, or a people group. Strongholds become problematic when they are demonically-influenced, manifesting as feelings of oppression, hopelessness, condemnation, lack of faith, deceit, and others. Satan uses diabolical strongholds in the lives of humanity to fulfill his assignment to kill, steal and destroy (John 10:10). The kingdom of darkness' overall goal is to destroy the life of an individual by any means necessary. An indicator of an authentic warfare intercessor is that they contend prayerfully and ask God to reveal the lies, mental images, and thought patterns of a deceived mind.

Some warfare intercessors have been anointed with spiritual perception to discern the evil spirits that reign over various territories. They have also been graced with strategies for establishing God's authority in places where the devil has taken both spiritual and physical ground. They fight from the place of a surrendered life to Holy Spirit (See Lesson 4). It is key that they dwell in the perpetual awareness that they must do nothing without the leading of Holy Spirit.

All intercessory types must also have intercessors covering them, or else they have no business functioning in any role especially spiritual warfare. The Warfare Intercessor must be a masterful steward of their body. It is of utmost importance to be spiritually, emotionally, and physically fit, have a mature devotional life with the word of God, and maintain a heart that is cleared from the debris of unforgiveness. When this type of Intercessor becomes weak, lazy, lethargic, and weary they are a diluted soldier who becomes a liability. Warfare Intercessors fight for those who have lost their capacity to follow Christ, they fight for the lost sheep (John 10:27-30; Luke 15:1-7) and those who do not have the strength to fight for themselves.

**RESEARCH INTERCESSORS** One area of warfare intercession is the area of "research intercession". These types of intercessors thrive on prayerfully collecting vital facts about strongholds and principalities. They help us formulate our plan of attack, also known as Spiritual Mapping (Jehoshaphat was a Warfare Intercessor).

### Hindrances for Warfare Intercessors

- Superman/Wonder Woman Complex: feeling like they are a one-man army. They believe that they can win the battle alone. They would sometimes come against principalities, and powers, of a certain place, or even the whole country ALONE.

- Seeing every moment of intercession as an opportunity to war and fight. The Warfare Intercessor can become so consumed with fighting, until they neglect resting in the

Lord and developing intimacy with Holy Spirit.

- Failing to refuel (spending time with the Lord). There are times we can move from fight to fight and never take time to recoup. It is okay to become quiet and to simply "be" in the presence of the Lord.

- There is a tendency that a warfare intercessor becomes overly aggressive in prayer that they would not give room for other people's gifts.

### Prophetic Intercessor

Prophetic Intercessors are individuals who have been chosen by God to have the gift of intercession *and* the gift of prophecy. They pray, pursue, and proclaim in prayer the things that are on the heart of God. Then under God's instruction, they release the words, thoughts, images and actions God has revealed to them. God speaks to prophetic intercessors in many ways: prayers, dreams, visions, songs, proclamations, symbolism and prophetic acts (See Lesson 2). Before anything occurs in the natural, it is first released in the spirit realm. These Intercessors are called to prepare the way for God's will to be done and released in the Earth.

To mature in this call, it demands that one be trustworthy of God's secrets even if it requires their reputation be bruised in the process. This type of intercession must be surrendered to God's authority and also God's delegated authority. Know that not every moment requires "a release", but sometimes the best thing the Prophetic Intercessor can do is function covertly. When the Holy Spirit is praying prophetically through one of His intercessors, the intent is always to protect, purify, and prosper His bride, the Church.

A prophetic intercessor who's not under God's delegated

authority, is ill-equipped to take a role of authority even in intercession (Hebrews 13:17). The heart of a prophetic intercessor is to see the unseen and to hear unheard things that God has for the person being prayed for to strengthen, edify, or comfort him or her.

<u>Hindrances for Prophetic Intercessors</u>

- Lack of submission to God's delegated authority. We do all things in decency and order (1 Corinthians 14:40).
- Toxic response to persecution, not everyone will willingly receive you or your words. Not every atmosphere, platform, or opportunity is tuned for what God has given you.
- Adding to or subtracting from what God has said in order to appear knowledgeable, or not ridiculous
- Finding identity in the gift, and not the One who GAVE the gift! So what, you are prophetic? Does the God of the Prophets KNOW YOU and do YOU KNOW Him?

# WHO ELSE IS CALLED TO INTERCESSION?

- **The Believer** Prayer/Intercession is the greatest technology of Heaven given to Humanity as a means to communicate with God. It is the Believers' right, and Heavens expectation that WE WOULD PRAY!!! It is our responsibility and means of utilizing our authority to call the will of God to Earth via our prayers and intercession (**Read: LUKE 11:1-13**)
    - **Hebrews 4:14-16 (NIV)** "Therefore, since we have a great high priest who has ascended into heaven, Jesus the Son of God, let us hold firmly to the faith

we profess. For we do not have a high priest who is unable to empathize with our weaknesses, but we have one who has been tempted in every way, just as we are—yet he did not sin. Let us then approach God's throne of grace with confidence, so that we may receive mercy and find grace to help us in our time of need."

- **The Desperate** Desperation has a language, a sound and a disposition to it that embodies faith and prayerfulness. The Desperate, in faith, posture and motives provides a space for God to be God in miraculous and merciful ways. Some examples are:
  - **The Woman with the Issue of Blood [Mark 5:21 - 43]**
    - Source of Desperation: vs 25-26
    - Act of Desperation: vs 27
    - Language of Desperation: vs 28
    - Results of Desperation: vs 29-34
  - **Father whose Son has an 'Impure Spirit'** [ M a r k 9:17-27]
    - Source of Desperation: vs 17-18
    - Act of Desperation: vs 20
    - Language of Desperation: vs 22-24
    - Results of Desperation: vs 25-26

# CELEBRATION ASSIGNMENT

"What type of intercessor am I really?"

Read through the list of the *12 Types of Intercessors* and complete the following:

1. Identify which area(s) best describe you and your experience with intercession.

2. Determine which description reflects the capacity in which you are called to serve in your church.

3. Develop a daily routine that you can commit "YOU" to for the next 21-days that reflects a type of Intercessor described in any one of the *12 Types of Intercessors*.

*Additional Note: Everything that You are...has been entrusted to you by Holy Spirit. If you are struggling to know what type(s) of Intercessor you are, employ Holy Spirit EVERY DAY for the next 21-days to clearly reveal to You who You are in Him.*

# NOTES

# MODULE FIVE

# BREAKING THE IMPASSE

The Types of Prayer

- What is an Impasse?
- Be like Rhoda
- Be INFORMED Intercessors
- 12 Types of Prayer

## PRAYER TARGET

The specific global, national, or local issue/person that you are burdened to cover for the next seven days. (Reference this chapter's celebration assignment). Employ Holy Spirit to take you deeper into various functions and areas of intercession.

## #MCBRIDEMOMENT

There are moments in the journey of Intercession, where the Individual does not have words or even desire to intercede and/or pray. These are dry moments, defined as impasses, that are truly divinely inspired. Romans 8 admonishes its readers that all things work together for the good of us who are called by God. Even the dry moments of prayer and God's silence are things that are working in our favor. The dry moments are only temporary and are actual catalysts to exponential growth if we choose to continue our pursuit of God despite what we are currently experiencing.

IMPASSE I im • pas I (noun) 1. a situation in which no progress is possible, especially because of disagreement; a deadlock. 2. A predicament affording no obvious escape

Within the context of Prayer and Intercession, **impasses** are seasons of prayerlessness characterized with feelings of stagnation, laziness, staleness, dryness, no fervor, and lack of excitement. This is the season in the journey of the Intercessor where we pray out of obligation or religion and not inspiration. There is no pull or no drive to 'pray onsite with insight'! This can be brought on by a number of factors: UNANSWERED Prayer, spiritual burnout, the NEED to go deeper in prayer, being in the WRONG environment(s), lack of knowledge understanding the Gift of Intercession (**Hosea 4:6**) and Satanic Attacks (**John 10:10**). We also hit moments of dryness, in our prayer lives, simply because the ANSWER is not packaged the way WE DESIRE or most familiar with!

In Acts 12 we are introduced to the story of Apostle Peter being arrested and placed on death row, simply for doing what God had commissioned him to do. Upon his arrest the Believers called a prayer gathering, with the expectation that God would hear and answer them by delivering the incarcerated Apostle.

While they prayed, Peter slept. The Bible tells us that God answered their prayer in the most supernatural and miraculous way. The Apostle is escorted out of the jail by an angelic being. He goes immediately to where the Saints were praying and believing God, to show them God heard and answered. However, upon his arrival, Peter was not greeted by a band of believers, he was greeted by a servant girl named Rhoda. What I love most about Rhoda's story is that she worked, prayed and watched for the answer. Here she is in a room full of seemingly mature people that had been walking with Peter for decades, being able to hear the answer to what they were praying for knocking at the door although she was immature. Those that were mature missed a moment of divine answer simply because they were not truly expecting God to deliver Apostle Peter to the door of their prayer meeting in the way God did.

Many of us are like this group of believers. We have been with God for so long that we are on autopilot in the way we expect God to show up. How many answers to prayer are we missing simply because of the way God chooses to package the answer? Be like Rhoda: working, praying, and watching! When the answer came, Rhoda got so excited, they told her she was crazy and confused. Her words were declared downright rubbish, but Rhoda remained indignant even in the face of the mature! She heard the answer to what they had been praying for! (**ALWAYS take the POSTURE of Rhoda - Acts 12:11-17.**)

KNOW that there is MORE than One way to PRAY and Intercede, just as there is MORE than ONE type of Intercessor! God always answers according to how we pray in a variety of ways as well! One thing that is consistent within the various types of Intercessor and types of Prayer is that the Individual praying MUST be INFORMED!

- **Devotional Life** Daily spend intentional time in the presence of God. This does not require us to speak, but it does require us to be present and aware of God's divine presence in our proximity. [Psalm 63:1-8]

- **Word Life** We are nothing without the Word of God! It is the life source of the faith we utilize when we pray [Romans 10:17]. Wherever the Word of the Lord is, there is also God's attention! Know that Heaven (eternity) and Earth (time) will pass away but it is the Word of God that will stand forever [Luke 21:33]. We must become masterfully skilled in knowing the written Word of God.

- **Research Life** Intercessors are informed people! We not only know the Word of God but we are highly aware of what is going on in our world and the systems that govern our experience. Please read a book, listen to podcasts, watch the news, study other cultures, travel, develop friendship with those who do not believe like you! All of these variables make us well informed intercessors who do not pray amiss [James 4:3, 2 Corinthians 2:11]. Yes, we gain direction on what to pray for by the empowerment of Holy Spirit, but we also gain intel simply because we are watchmen who are informed.

- **Private Life** Your anointing is only as powerful as the private life you prescribe to! Who we are in secret always flows out of us in everything we do. Never be so committed to a perfect public image that private life becomes a mausoleum we have made our dwelling place. Intercessors often attempt to do with faith what God has given us the power to do practically! The word is true, "For just as the body without the spirit is dead, so also faith without works is dead" #noPublicSUCCESSandPrivateFAILURE

- **Practice Makes Perfect** Prayer, Intercession, Fasting and commissioning Faith are all disciplines that require focus. Everything about our flesh is going to fight against our decision to operate in any of these [Romans 7:18] but know that the more we engage in these the stronger we become. Take time to practice praying...no prayer is wasted!

We learned to properly communicate by engaging in conversations and practicing the use of words. So, it is with praying, the more we do it the more competent and versed we become.

Biblically, there are several noticeable approaches to Prayer and Intercession that are all interchangeable throughout the text but are often times missed:

- Apostle Paul-THANKSGIVING
  - Romans 1:8
  - 1 Corinthians 1:4
  - Ephesians 1:16
- David - PRAISE, Exaltation
  - Psalm 8:1
  - Psalm 18:2
  - Psalm 103:1-2
- Joshua - Mindfulness of God's Word and Promises
  - Joshua 1:8

It is interesting that at different phases of their life experiences, men and women engaged in various forms of prayer that not only produced results but also gained God's attention. I personally believe that God responds to humanity because of who we are to Him but also because of who God is to us [Psalm 34:17]. However, it is undeniable that our petitions, requests, words, and even objectives in prayer all have purpose to the audience of Heaven.

I have listed what I believe are 12 types of prayer, though in no way do I believe this to be an exhaustive list. However, this list serves the purpose of identifying modes and types of prayer that we should be intentional about exploring. When you pray, always ensure that it is sincere and intimate, where both you and God can be fully heard, seen, and felt, knowing that prayer is just as much speaking as it is listening.

## 12 TYPES OF PRAYER

### 1. Praise
The Act of Declaring YOUR lived TRUTH about WHO God is, WHAT God has done, and WHAT God will do simply because God promised. Praise lifts the burden of heaviness, but it also keeps humanity mindful of God's character.

**Biblical Character:** Apostle Peter
**Scripture:** 1 Peter 1:3-9 (NIV) "Praise be to the God and Father of our Lord Jesus Christ! In his great mercy he has given us new birth into a living hope through the resurrection of Jesus Christ from the dead, and into an inheritance that can never perish, spoil or fade. This inheritance is kept in heaven for you, who through faith are shielded by God's power until the coming of the salvation that is ready to be revealed in the last time. In all this you greatly rejoice, though now for a little while you may have had to suffer grief in all kinds of trials. These have come so that the proven genuineness of your faith—of greater worth than gold, which perishes even though refined by fire—may result in praise, glory and honor when Jesus Christ is revealed. Though you have not seen him, you love him; and even though you do not see him now, you believe in him and are filled with an inexpressible and glorious joy, for you are receiving the end result of your faith, the salvation of your souls."

### 2. Agreement
The form of Intercession where multiple people agree on Earth for what Heaven is saying and HAS ALREADY SAID about a

specific person, place, or thing. It is the Law of Agreement in full manifestation.

**Biblical Character:** The Acts Church
**Scripture:** Acts 12 and Matthew 18:19-20 (NIV) "Again, truly I tell you that if two of you on earth agree about anything they ask for, it will be done for them by my Father in heaven. For where two or three gather in my name, there am I with them."

### 3. Thanksgiving

The act of offering thanks to God, simply for being God and/or for acts of benevolence (mercy, joy, love, salvation, giving, etc). Thanksgiving consistently reminds the Believer that the faith of Christianity is a thinking theology. It is impossible to give thanks and not pause to think or reflect. Most of the letters Apostle Paul wrote, he continuously thanked God for the lives of those he had the grace to affect. NEVER lose your capacity to express gratitude for what God has given.

**Biblical Character:** Apostle Paul
**Scripture:** 2 Corinthians 2:14-16 and 1 Thessalonians 5:18 (NIV) "Give thanks in all circumstances; for this is God's will for you in Christ Jesus."

### 4. Praying the Bible

Praying the scriptures as your personal prayer. This is where devotional life and having a word life collide together. It is impossible to pray what we have not taken time to become accustomed to. It is the art of meditating on the Word of God [Psalm 1], permitting God's word to come alive from the book into your reality.

**Biblical Character:** Prophet Daniel
**Scripture:** Daniel 9 [ref. Jeremiah 25:1-11]

## 5. Confession

(a) Acknowledging personal sin to God, and then celebrating the forgiveness that has already been provided through the death, burial and resurrection of Jesus. (b) The act of declaring the Word of God (prophecies & written Word of God) over seemingly insurmountable situations. We confess the Word of God before we permit ourselves to complain or drown in trepidation.

**Biblical Character:** David
**Scripture:** Psalm 51:2-3 (NKJV) "Wash me thoroughly from my iniquity, And cleanse me from my sin. For I acknowledge my transgressions, and my sin is always before me."

## 6. Fellowship

Spending intentional time with God, with no agenda other than to simply experience God. It has the familiarity of two longtime friends conversing with each other. [We are the Friend of God, ref. Module 1]

**Biblical Character:** Adam and Eve
**Verse:** Genesis 3:8 (AMP) "And they heard the sound of the Lord God walking in the garden in the cool [afternoon breeze] of the day, so the man and his wife hid and kept themselves hidden from the presence of the Lord God among the trees of the garden. But the Lord God called to Adam, and said to him, "Where are you?" He said, "I heard the sound of You [walking] in the garden, and I was afraid because I was naked; so, I hid myself."

## 7. Listening

Also known as 'soaking', it is an act of intimacy with God, where the individual simply sits at the feet of Jesus listening to

Him. It is sometimes accompanied with music, but I imagine that when Mary sat at Jesus' feet there was no music playing. When we sit in the presence of the Lord and simply listen, we are permitting God to speak to us. This is a moment to gain clarity, direction, wisdom, healing, closure and sobriety to the heart. Most people find this mode of prayer to be difficult because it requires focus and the self-discipline to be still in God's presence.

**Biblical Character:** Mary of Bethany
**Scripture:** Luke 10:38-42

### 8. Intercession
Prayers that are Spirit-led, sanctioning Heaven on the behalf of a person, place, thing, or cause.

**Biblical Character:** Anna
**Scripture:** Luke 2:36-37 (CSB) "There was also a prophetess, Anna, a daughter of Phanuel, of the tribe of Asher. She was well along in years, having lived with her husband seven years after her marriage, and was a widow for eighty-four years. She did not leave the temple, serving God night and day with fasting and prayers."

### 9. Petition
Seeing a need and praying for it. As aforementioned in Lesson 4, prayer is directed from Earth to Heaven, talking to God about Earth matters this is petitioning.

**Biblical Character:** Jesus
**Scripture:** Luke 11:5-9

### 10. Praying in Tongues
Utilizing a **personal** spiritual language that edifies the individual

praying and also their relationship with God. It is the act of permitting Holy Spirit to intercede and pray through us, via our heavenly language being manifested.

**Biblical Character:** Apostle Paul
**Scripture:** Jude 20-21 and 1 Corinthians 14:14 (AMP) "One who speaks in a tongue **edifies** himself; but one who prophesies **edifies** the church [promotes growth in spiritual wisdom, devotion, holiness, and joy]."

## 11. Prophetic

(a) Gaining confidential information from Heaven concerning a person, place, or thing and specifically targeting that thing to be made manifest via the vehicle of prayer. (b) Receiving a message in prayer to relay to a person.

**Biblical Character:** Jeremiah
**Scripture:** Jeremiah 1:7

## 12. Warfare

Confronting the kingdom of Satan with the weapons of God's Kingdom, ultimately preparing the way for the Glory of God.

**Biblical Character:** The 72 other Apostles commissioned and sent by Jesus
**Scripture:** Luke 10:1-2 and Ephesians 6:10-13 (AMP) "In conclusion, be strong in the Lord [draw your strength from Him and be empowered through your union with Him] and in the power of His [boundless] might. Put on the full armor of God [for His precepts are like the splendid armor of a heavily armed soldier], so that you may be able to [successfully] stand up against all the schemes and the strategies and the deceits of the devil. For our struggle is not against flesh and blood [contending only with physical opponents], but against the

rulers, against the powers, against the world forces of this [present] darkness, against the spiritual forces of wickedness in the heavenly (supernatural) places. Therefore, put on the complete armor of God, so that you will be able to [successfully] resist and stand your ground in the evil day [of danger], and having done everything [that the crisis demands], to stand firm [in your place, fully prepared, immovable, victorious]."

# CELEBRATION ASSIGNMENT

"Pray through it?"

Matched with the Homework assignment from Lesson 4 and your '21-day Plan' to grow in your specific identity as an Intercessor, connect with a global/national issue to intercede for over the next 7 days. Document what Heaven shares with you! (Example: Soul Intercessor using Praying the Bible, begin praying 2 Peter 3:9 over an unbeliever who has major influence in one of the systems of our world, for the next 7-days).

*Additional Note: This assignment requires you to be informed, so research is a must.*

# NOTES

# MODULE SIX

# TOOLS & WEAPONS OF THE INTERCESSOR

part one

- Fasting
- The Groan
- Despair vs. Desperation

## PRAYER TARGET

Joel 2:28 "And afterward I will pour out My Spirit upon all flesh; and your sons and your daughters shall prophesy, your old men shall dream dreams, your young men shall see visions." We are asking for an outpouring of God's spirit on us individually for the sake of us being catalysts for revival and restoration. We are expecting the glory of the Lord to be expanded in every facet of our lives, so that we can understand God in a greater way. [Habakkuk 2:14].

## #MCBRIDEMOMENT

As an Intercessor, a person of faith, and a Believer in the Body of Christ, ensure that you safeguard yourself from faith malpractice because you are ill prepared or misinformed about the tools and weapons God has invested into us. Our faith tools are not meant to be used for the sake of bending the will of God or humanity, but our tools are to be used to bring us into divine alignment to hear God and silence the toxic nature of our flesh.

**Fasting** is an ancient technology that people have used across cultures for several millennia. Fasting is essentially the act of abstaining from a thing, for an extended period of time, as an act of discipline. It enables the person fasting to gain focus, naturally heal, and tap deeper into their spiritual being. From a biblical perspective men and women from both the Old and New Testaments engaged in fasting. Fasting brought them closer to God, into divine alignment with God's will, but it also brought them to the place of answers when their reality seemed awry.

In Matthew 17:14-21, the disciples asked Jesus why they could not heal the child that was demonically-oppressed. Jesus responded, "Because of your unbelief...howbeit THIS kind of demon does not go out except by prayer and fasting." Unbelief disables our ability to dislodge diabolical strongholds, it causes us to be blinded even to the presence of demonic strongholds. Know that it takes faith to overcome the enemy and take territories where he has erected strongholds.

Fasting assists us in incapacitating unbelief and establishing resilient faith. **Faith** needs prayer for its development and full growth, but **prayer** needs fasting for the same reason. Fasting has and can-do wonders when used in combination with prayer and faith. **All** Believers of Christ are to fast. However, there are no regulations or set rules given to for how long or how often. This is where obedience and discernment MUST be facilitated to listen to the voice of God, but overall, it is determined by the individual's desire and need.

## What does Fasting, as a spiritual practice, do?

- Humbles the Soul before the Lord: **Psalm 35:13 (AMP)**
- Chastens the Soul: **Psalm 69:10 (KJV)**

- Aids in temptation: **Matthew 4:1-11**

- Crucifies and denies appetites to give strength to FOCUS in prayer: **2 Samuel 12:16-23**

- It manifests earnestness for God, and exclusion for all else. The act of abstaining signifies that nothing else can satisfy us the way God can. Fasting is an ultimate demonstration of discipline: **1 Corinthians 7:5**

- Develops Faith, CRUCIFIES unbelief, helps to attain power over demons, and aids in prayer: **Matthew 17:14-21**

| INDIVIDUAL FASTING | CORPORATE FASTING |
|---|---|
| Jesus (40 days) **Matthew 4:1-11** | Samuel and Israel **1 Samuel 7:5-6** |
| Joshua with Moses (40 days) **Exodus 24:13-18** | Joel & Tribe of Judah **Joel 2:15-18** |
| Daniel (21 days) **Daniel 10:2-14** | Ezra & Levites **Ezra 8:21-23** |
| Paul and 276 Men (14 days) **Acts 27:33-34** | City of Nineveh **Jonah 3** |
| David (7 days) **2 Samuel 12:7-23** | Tribe of Judah **2 Chronicles 20:1-27** |

Notice that from this list every person that fasted for an extended period of time faced a situation that required something that ONLY God could do. In most cases, these people CHOSE to sacrifice something (**becoming living sacrifices**) so that other generations and people could live, but also so that God's promises and KINGDOM could be made manifest on the Earth. Fasting is about becoming a walking, living, breathing sacrifice (Romans 12:1-3), putting self in a place of vulnerability so that God can move THROUGH and FOR us.

**Corporate Fasting** is when a group of people come together, in agreement, having ONE voice, ONE mind, operating in

ONE Spirit to abstain from pleasure so that God can intervene in Earth's matters. It is the power and manifestation of the *Law of Agreement* **Matthew 18:20.** Fasting is also a weapon of deliverance. According to **Isaiah 58:6,** liberty comes when fasting is utilized. Bear in mind that authentic fasting is healthy, it produces focus and clarity that brings the person fasting into divine alignment with the will of God.

Even as we practice faith by operating in prayer, intercession, fasting and giving, we must consistently be mindful that God is sovereign. God does what God wants to, however, whenever, and wherever God chooses to do so. No one can bend God's hand; He is not a genie that grants wishes when rubbed the right way. There are two types of fast:

- FULL FAST: No food or water (however water is suggested) **Esther 4:13-17; Esther 5-8**
- PARTIAL FAST: From Sunup to Sundown (can be Full Fast or Daniel Fast) **Daniel 6:18-24**

Fasting is valuable whether you are engaging in a full or partial fast. One day fasts help to fortify and edify our spirit when done on a consistent basis (i.e. taking every Friday to partially/fully fast can be exceptionally beneficial as opposed to not fasting at all). It builds discipline in preparation for fasts with longer durations of time. Fasting for a continual 72-hours with nothing but water is a profound way to see revolution and deliverance take place [Esther 4]. Know that fasting without devotion is nothing more than a diet! When you fast, be intentional and aggressive with spending time with God.

**Groaning,** also known as travailing, is another ancient technology Heaven has invested into humanity. We are first introduced to the groan in Exodus 2:23-25, after the death of

Joseph and before the birth of Moses. The Children of Israel were in bondage under an Egyptian ruler who had not heard of the great exploits their ancestor did for the dynasty. They were foreigners in a now strange land, and as a result of their oppression, the scripture presents that they groaned and sighed as well as cried out for help.

We are told that God heard their groaning, and as a result God remembered the covenant sworn to their ancestor Abraham. God saw them from the place of that covenant. God took notice and was concerned about them. Immediately after they groaned, Moses was commissioned by God to go back to Egypt as a deliverer speaking on God's behalf. The people groaned and God was mandated to respond to His Word sworn to their ancestor about them.

Wherever the eyes of the Lord are, there is God's Word (Jeremiah 1:12), but there is also the safety of God (Matthew 24:35). The groan is only appropriate when things have been a certain way for a long time. Groans come out of people and churches when things have not changed. Desperation, deprivation, and hunger are all results from the lack of change. However, the lack of change is often the strategy of Heaven. God knows the POWER OF WAIT and how it deepens our desire for manifestation.

I have come to realize there is a dynamic difference between despair and desperation; we essentially choose how we engage our present adversity.

- **Despair**- complete loss or absence of hope, the act of being without hope
- **Desperation**- a state of despair that results in rash or extreme behavior

**Despair** is a mindset that disempowers its host from action. Where there is despair, there is no hope and where there is no hope, there is no Christ (Colossians 1:27). Desperation is manifested when we resort to behaviors with no regard for consequences. The nameless Woman in Luke 8 saw that Jesus was on His way to Jairus' house to heal his daughter, but she had a need that required Christ's intervention. The text tells us that she pressed through the crowd, not to stir attention to herself, but to simply touch the lowest part of Jesus' garment because her faith said touching Him would heal her.

When you study the historical cultural context of this scripture, you will discover that the Woman put herself at risk of stoning. For twelve years, she dealt with this issue in her body and no one could help her. I can imagine her desperation for relief drove her to risk it all just to see Jesus.

Despair and strong desperation are the only options we have while we are waiting on the Lord! God **delivers** from despair and depression, but God **drives** us to desperation. Desperation is the force behind the miraculous, supernatural things that occur. It is the posture that says, "God IF You do not come through...this WILL BE the end." Groaning essentially converts anguish into expectation! Behind every prayer there is a capacity, weight, and depth to release a groan. With the right circumstances, right emergency, right issue comes a shift in the Intercessor's prayer life.

Pain is oftentimes a vehicle of choice that Heaven uses to shift and birth the Intercessor. Pain is the universal language of humanity, and it can either be converted into a groan or a snare! This has everything to do with heart posture, maturity, and initial response. Groaning comes when anguish and pain have been converted into expectation that says, "This cannot be the end of me". Expectation reflects faith, which is the epicenter of humanity's ability to please God (Hebrew 11:6). I believe God becomes grieved when we DO NOT 'expect' Him, especially when we have history with God. The Groan locates the promises of God and causes the people to become priority to God's focus. The groan is the highest level of communication Earth has with Heaven.

## WHO GROANS?

- **ALL of Creation** <u>Romans 8:22-23 (NIV)</u>: "We know that the whole creation has been groaning as in the pains of childbirth right up to the present time. Not only so, but we ourselves, who have the first fruits of the Spirit, groan inwardly as we wait eagerly for our adoption to sonship, the redemption of our bodies."

Groaning is permitting Jesus the Intercessor, who is consistently praying for us, to intercede/pray through us. (**Romans 8:34** and **Hebrews 7:25**)

- **Jesus** <u>John 11:33 (KJV)</u>: "When Jesus therefore saw her weeping, and the Jews also weeping which came with her, he groaned in the spirit, and was troubled."

If JESUS groaned, surely, WE will too! Jesus was 100% God but also 100% Man. If He, in His earthly divinity, groaned due to a life circumstance, we will too. Jesus' groan reached a vibration and intensity at the mouth of Lazarus' grave that resurrection was the principal result.

- God put the groan on Earth to get His attention when nothing else works (prayers of supplication, petitions, etc). All of creation groans. It is the unified language of everything created including the Heavens. The groan is the exclamation point of 'prayer'.

The power of response is your responsibility, not God's. Intercessors make sure that your response to life's adversity is producing revival and not revolt. Revival produces change to systems, worlds and lives that others can build upon, as well as sustain. Because revival is smothered in reformation, without it, revival would be nothing but covert pride. However, revolt is destructive; it is self-serving with an agenda that is individual focused and not communal.

When we are being positioned to having our personal and/ or corporate prayer lives deepened, God will place His hand on our reactions and responses. Many of us give our responses to Satan. Our level and type of response reflects our level of maturity in the Spirit! In moments of disagreement, we develop Spirits of the Vagabond. We wander from place to place, church to church, people to people, relationships to relationships because we do not know how to respond well. If we respond with carnality, we miss out on the opportunity for the Groan to do what it is supposed to do: **grasp God's attention to REMEMBER!**

The right response gives access to reward and part of responding well is realizing NOT EVERYTHING REQUIRES A RESPONSE! Sometimes silence is the appropriate response! When Pharaoh died in Exodus the Hebrews did not respond in revolt, they responded with a groan!

Revolt and Revival sound the same without apostolic graces and authorities soberly giving order and direction. Revolts advance people, but revival advances the Kingdom of God! Their Groaning caused God to 'remember' them, produce a Deliverer (Moses), and ultimately manifest glory for the sake of their deliverance (Exodus 6-11).

Know that God is concerned about the bondage of ALL people! The Groan is what keeps the fire and zeal of deliverance within a ministry burning hot. The MORE YOU GROAN, the MORE AGGRESSIVE GOD BECOMES to FREE the People!

# CELEBRATION ASSIGNMENT

"Lord, this is too much!"

Take three days to extensively reflect on your life. Go back to your earliest memory and work your way back to present day. Take an assessment of your decisions that have negatively affected your life. Identify where you are holding grudges, offenses, and even levels of unforgiveness against yourself. Employ Holy Spirit to show you the things about yourself that you have to release You from. Once you have taken inventory, write them down and for the next 7 days fast and groan in the presence of the Lord concerning yourself.

**Additional Notes:** We are the first partakers of the pour we carry. Far too often, the Intercessor places his or her own inner healing on the backburner while we spend intentional time laboring for other people. The ultimate knowledge is self-knowledge, because it brings you into the awareness that you cannot best serve anyone else if you do not know who you are first.

# NOTES

# MODULE SEVEN

# TOOLS & WEAPONS OF THE INTERCESSOR

part two

- Praise
- Identity
- Angels
- Community

- The Word of God
- The Blood of Jesus
- Binding and Loosing

## PRAYER TARGET

We pray that God brings us into a greater awareness of who He is in every facet of our lives! We employ Holy Spirit to teach us who God has been, who God is and how God desires to manifest Himself to humanity. We pray, "Holy Spirit, make me more AWARE. Make me sensitive to the identity of the True and Living God. **Hosea 4:6 (NLT)** "My people are being destroyed because they don't know me. Since you priests refuse to know me, I refuse to recognize you as my priests. Since you have forgotten the laws of your God, I will forget to bless your children.""

## #MCBRIDEMOMENT

When we are introduced to the transformative power of the Gospel, it not only renovates us spiritually, but it also illuminates how we should see ourselves and our Creator God. God's investment of tools and weapons into humanity, to enact our God-given victory over the affairs of Earth and Heaven, are all indicators that we are invaluable to God.

Each tool is readily available and accessible to the Believer, but ignorance often keeps us lulled in darkness. The use of these tools and weapons reproduce honor and gratitude that is shown from the user (the Believer) to the manufacturer (God).

**Praise** is another ancient technology that Heaven has invested into humanity. It is highly effective when utilized with the Divine as its chief focus. According to **Psalm 8:1-2 (NIV)** God has His praises in the mouths of humanity to essentially establish strongholds against the enemy but also to silence him. Why are both Praise, Worship, and Intercession dually used to bring us closer to God but also a weapon against the kingdom of darkness?

- Reminds Satan of Defeat
- Invites God to inhabit a particular situation and/or space
- Gives Strength and Hope
- Shifts focus to what authentically matters
- Reminds the Believer of God's Promises

In 2 Chronicles 20, we see the war tactics produced when praise, worship and intercession are utilized. The Tribe of Judah never lifted a weapon to fight, but they lifted their lives, bodies, voices and hearts. God dwelled in their praises and confounded their would-be enemies in such a way that they destroyed each other and left spoils for the people of Judah to reap.

**Identity** is a phenomenal weapon but can also be destructive when not managed correctly. Realizing who we are and whose we are postures us for living; realization is illuminating. Knowledge can either save your life or make you pay for a lifetime, severely. The pursuit of it is the ultimate determinant of where you will land. It makes sense that the scripture admonishes us to seek first the Kingdom of God and all other things will be added (Matthew 6:33). Seeking is sobering as well as enriching. Know that the art of seek will never go unsatisfied. Knowledge of our identity in Christ should be the mediator by which we govern ourselves.

Ephesians 2 tells us that we are seated in the Heavens in Christ Jesus. His seat is a direct result of His victory, won at Calvary. Christ is seated in eternal perpetual victory, nothing can move Him and as a result of Him being seated in victory, we too are seated as well. Know that wherever Christ is seated we too are there! It is with this type of knowledge that we should face life and actively pursue all that it righteously offers.

Knowledge keeps us from believing that someone else's life is worth our own. The first order of knowledge is self-knowledge, it is the place from which the questions *who are you, what are you made of, from whom do you come, and who sent you* originate. Our names are simply nothing more than an identifier; it is not who we are. When we come into the awareness of who we are, we descend from our self-imposed altars of sacrifice and we sit in our rightful place in Christ. The illuminating force of knowledge obliterates every idol-manifested as a savior complex.

**Angels** from a biblical historical perspective have been an intricate part of humanity's narrative both in Heaven and Earth. We are introduced to them, some believe, in Genesis during creation. It is implied that they assisted God in the making of male and female begins (Genesis 1:26-27). Angels worked with Old Testament Prophets (2 Kings 6:16-20), but they also ensured the safety of entire kingdoms (Judges 6:11-23). In the New Testament, they announced the coming of

Emmanuel to numerous people (Luke 1:26-56 & Luke 2:8-20). They ensured Christ's safety as a child (Matthew 2), but they also strengthened Him at the beginning of His ministerial journey (Matthew 4). They dynamically helped the forefathers of the Christian Church spoken of in Acts (Acts 1:10-11, Acts 5, Acts 12). They give insight and comfort as it pertains to heavenly affairs, granting revelatory insight to the Apostle John (Revelation 5). In the life of the Believer, angels have functions that many of us are unaware of.

- **Bring answers to prayer and direction** (Daniel 9:20-23 & Acts 10:1-6)

- **Protectors of Believers** (Psalm 34)

- **Gathering the Elected of God** (Matthew 24:31 & Revelation 7:1-3)

- **Binding the Enemy** (Revelations 20:1-3)

- **Minister to Believers** (Hebrews 1:14 & Matthew 4:11)

- **Execute God's judgement**

Angels, just like Holy Spirit, should be employed and released to fulfill the will of God in our lives.

**Community** is of absolute importance in the life and longevity of Intercessors. Who we are is just as important as who we permit ourselves to be connected to. There will be life moments in our narratives that will place pressure on our need for healthy community. Community is where we righteously unpack and process through our inner wars. There will be instances where we will not have the wherewithal to pray or even believe God for ourselves. This is where the strength of community is mandatory. It is true, an authentic friend loves at all times, but a brother is born to share adversity (Proverbs

17:17). The right community reminds us of our identity in God, but they also assist in safeguarding who we are. Overall, our community helps us to fight the fight of faith but also thrive in the victory God has granted us (Ecclesiastes 4:9-12).

**The Word of God** is an amazing tool and weapon given to the Believer. Here is why:

- WHEREVER there is Word, there is also God's active power and BEINGNESS
  - **Jeremiah 1:12 (AMPC)**
  - **John 1:1 (ICB)**
  - **Numbers 23:19 (AMPC)**
- WHEREVER there is Word, there is also God's providence
  - **Deuteronomy 8:3 (NKJV)**
- WHEREVER there is the Word of God, there we also have the FINAL authority.
  - **Matthew 5:18 (VOICE)**
- WHEREVER there is the Word of God, we also have the NAME of God. Having the Name of God permits us to experience God by that name. (SEE Names of God List at end of Chapter).

**The Blood of Jesus** is probably the greatest tool God has invested into humanity simply because it is our propitiation back to all that was originally intended for humanity before the naphal. When we begin to plead the blood of Jesus, know that this is not a delusory claim of a magical formula of words. However, when we plead the Blood of Jesus over a specific person, place, or thing, a spiritual dynamic is initiated.

The authority of the blood of Jesus far exceeds any energy or source that any human or demonic force could ever employ. Just as the shed of Jesus Christ brought about redemption, it also delivers, discharges, and deactivates the operations of hell and the frailties of the flesh. Know that it is expected that every believer in Christ appropriates and legislates the blood in tough situations, as an intervention of manifesting God's will.

The origin of Passover gives the greater revelation to our faith's dependency on the Blood of Jesus. In Israel's deliverance from the last plague of Egypt, in which the firstborn of every family was doomed to die, the Israelites were instructed by God to place the blood of a lamb on their doorposts and lintels, so that the plague of His judgment would "pass over" their houses. **Exodus 12:13-14:** "Now the blood **shall be a sign for you on the houses where you are.** And when I see the blood, **I will pass over you; and the plague shall not be on you to destroy you** when I strike the land of Egypt. So, **this day shall be to you a memorial;** and you shall keep it as a feast to the Lord throughout your generations." I believe the Blood of Jesus does four specific things. It:

- Protects
- Delivers
- Removes Hopelessness, by providing a new day
- Gives Witness to the Promises of God [Hebrews 12:24]

**Binding and Loosing** are described by Christ as being the keys to the kingdom (Matthew 16:19). Binding in this text is the Greek word *deo*, meaning:

- To Tie/Fasten/Knit/Wind with chains or to throw into chains

- To put under obligation of law

- To prohibit, forbid, to declare to be illicit (illegitimate, criminal, felonious, banned, outlawed, unauthorized, and unsanctioned)

- To be bound to one (wife/husband nuptials...the two are bound together as one)

- To irrevocably place under legal obligation.

It means to essentially prohibit undesirable spiritual activities, as you would if you were issuing a restraining order. Satan is legally obligated to observe all terms and agreements as outlined by us, the issuer, within our prayers. If we say nothing, we permit hell to do whatever it desires, even if that means our very demise. The scripture admonishes us to take charge and command our mornings. We have the capacity to shake hell out of its holding place in the affairs of Earth and our lives (Job 38:12). Just as much as binding can resist and apprehend, we often forget that it permits us to apprehend. Intercessors, a powerful prayer to pray is, "*Lord, I bind my heart to Yours. May my heart be synchronized to the beating and pace of Yours, so that I may never step ahead of You or stray from the path of righteousness.*"

To loose is also profound when utilized in the life of a person of faith. Loosing in this text is the Greek word *lyo* meaning:

- To loose any person or thing tied or fastened as One to another thing (nullifying relationships)

- To unbind, release from bonds, to set free, to discharge from prison to let go (removal of bandages, breaking chains, to break down, to break up)

- To undo, dissolve anything bound, tied or compacted together, to melt away (dismiss, break-up, annul, demolish, overthrow, to away with)

- To unloose and release
- To emancipate or release from an assignment, contracted activities/post, or undesirable state of confinement or imprisonment.

Know that our identity in God enables us to release demonic and satanic spirits from all destructive, deadly and lethal assignments given by Satan. We can circumvent all things that are contrary to the will of God pertaining to our reality. Do not ever hesitate to utilize the weapons: fasting, groaning, identity, community, angels, the Blood of Jesus, binding and loosing.

# CELEBRATION ASSIGNMENT

"There is power in His Name and His Word."

- For the next 7 days, pray through 7 names of God. Select any seven from the list below. I would also suggest pulling on your history with God. How has God revealed Godself to you? Call on God by that name too...

- Specifically target a certain issue, person, place or thing praying God's name and word about it. Example: Jehovah 'Ori: The Lord my Light, according to your identity and promise give me light and clarity concerning the decisions I should make with my career. You are my light; I trust You to show me the way I should go.

# NOTES

## TOOLS & WEAPONS OF THE INTERCESSOR (part two)

# NAMES OF GOD

**I AM THAT I AM** Personal name in the original form spoken by God to Moses in Exodus 3:14. I am is the shortest name mentioned by God. YHWH is the strictest form in Hebrew without vowels.

**YAHWEH** Hebrew YHWH with vowels, means Lord

**JEHOVAH** Means which is (present), which was (past), which shall be (future)

**JAH JEHOVAH** The Lord Jehovah

**ADONI JAH** Jehovah is Lord

**ADONI/ADONAI** Lord expressing divine dominion; means master or owner. Authority, power, deity, reverence, relationship, responsibility, master, sir. Means sovereign Psalm 147:5; 86:12

**ADONAI JEHOVAH SABOATH** Master, Lord of Host Psalm 69:6

**JEHOVAH ELOHIM** The majestic Omnipotent God Zechariah 13:9; Psalm 118:27

**JEHOVAH ELOHIM SABOATH** Lord God of Hosts. Hosts of heaven creation and creatures Psalm 84:8, Jeremiah 15:16

**JAH ELOHIM** Lord God Psalm 68:18

**JEHOVAH BARA** Lord Creator Isaiah 40:28

**JEHOVAH CHATSAHI** the Lord my strength Psalm 27:1

**JEHOVAH CHERUB** Lord the sword Deuteronomy 33:29

**JEHOVAH ELEON** The Lord the blesser

**JEHOVAH ELI** Lord my God Psalm 18:2

**JEHOVAH ELOHAY** Lord my God. My Lord. Divine sovereignty personal faith in the God of Power Judges 13:8

**JEHOVAH ELOHEENU** Lord our God. What He is, where He

is, what he said, what he did, what He gave, what He has, what He shows Psalm 99:5

**JEHOVAH ELOHEKA** Lord thy God. Denotes Jehovah's relationship to His people and the responsibility to Him Four truths go with name. Redemption, relationship, responsibility, and reward of the Lord Deuteronomy 2:7

**JEHOVAH ELYON** The Lord Most High Psalm 7:17

**JEHOVAH GADOR MILCHAMAH** The Lord Mighty in Battle Psalm 24:8

**JEHOVAH GANAN** The Lord Our Defense Psalm 89:18

**JEHOVAH GMOLAH** The God of Recompenses. Vengeance belongs to God not humanity Deuteronomy 32:35

**JEHOVAH GO'EL** The Lord my Redeemer Isaiah 49:26; 60:16

**JEHOVAH HAMELECH** The Lord my King Psalm 98:6

**JEHOVAH HELECH 'OLAM** The Lord, King forever Psalm 10:6

**JEHOVAH HOSEENU** The Lord Our Maker, we are God's workmanship Psalm 95:6

**JEHOVAH HOSHE'AH** The Lord who saves Psalm 20:9

**JEHOVAH IMMEKU** The Lord who is with you Judges 6:12

**JEHOVAH IZOA HAKABOTH** Lord strong and mighty Psalm 24:8

**JEHOVAH JIREH** The Lord who Provides, God always provides for what He commands from His people Genesis 22:14

**JEHOVAH KANNA** The Jealous Lord Exodus 34:14

` Horn of salvation Psalm 18:2

**JEHOVAH KUBODHI** The Lord my glory Psalm 3:3

**JEHOVAH LAMI** The Lord my Strength Psalm 28:7

**JEHOVAH MACHSI** The Lord my refuge Psalm 91:9

**JEHOVAH MAGEN** The Lord my Shield Deuteronomy 33:29

**JEHOVAH MAKKEH** The Lord our Discipliner Ezekiel 7:9

**JEHOVAH MA'OZ** Lord my fortress Jeremiah 16:19

**JEHOVAH M'KADDESH** The Lord my Sanctifier Exodus 31:13, 1 Corinthians 1:30

**JEHOVAH MEPHALTI** The Lord my deliverer Psalm 18:2

**JEHOVAH METSHODHATHI** The Lord my fortress Psalm 18:2

**JEHOVAH MISQABBI** Lord my High tower Psalm 18:2

**JEHOVAH NISSI** The Lord our Banner. Nissi means a standard, ensign, sign or pole Psalm 20:5; 60:4

**JEHOVAH 'ORI** The Lord my Light Psalm 27:1

**JEHOVAH RAAH** The Lord my Shepherd Psalm 23:1

**JEHOVAH ROPHI/RAPHA** The Lord the physician/healer Psalm 103:3; 147:3

**JEHOVAH SEL'I** The Lord my Rock Psalm 18:2

**JEHOVAH SHALOM** The Lord our peace and wealth, good health, all is well, safe prosperity, favour, rest, finished, full, whole, make good, restitution or repay, perfect. The giver of satisfaction Judges 6:24

**JEHOVAH SHAMMAH** The Lord is there (present) Ezekiel 48:35, Hebrews 13:5

**JEHOVAH SHAPHAT** The Lord our Judge Judges 11:27

**JEHOVAH TSEBAAH** The Lord of Hosts. Host means warfare or service. Divine master or controller. Tsebaoth means armies. The Lord of hosts is divine revelation and authority! The eternal God of Armies 1 Samuel 1:3

**JEHOVAH TSIDKENU** The Lord our righteousness Jeremiah 23:6

**JEHOVAH 'UZAM** The Lord my strength in trouble Isaiah 49:26

**ELOHIM** The 1st name of God. Showing God's power, might and authority in trium form (God the Father, Son Holy Spirit)

**EL** the singular form of Elohim, meaning strong One. Great, mighty, dreadful, and almighty. It reveals the singleness of each being in the Godhead. God the Father as El Genesis 14:18-22, God the Son as El Isaiah 7:14; 9:6; Psalm 22:1 and 89:26, God the Holy Spirit as El Job 33:4; 37:10

**BEN ELOHIM** The Son of God Matthew 16:16, 26:63. John 6:69

**EL AMAN** The faithful God Deuteronomy 7:9

**EL BEYTHEL** God of Bethel/ God of the House of God Genesis 31:13

**EL CHAYIM** The Living God Joshua 3:10

**EL ELOHE ISRAEL** God of Israel Genesis 33:20

**EL ELYOWN** God most High. The Highest Genesis 14:19

**EL ROI** The God who sees Me

**EL SHADDAY** God Almighty

**EL OLAM** The Eternal God

**EL CHAY** Living God

**ADVOCATE** 1 John 2:1

**ALMIGHTY** Revelation 1:8; Matthew 28:18

**ALPHA AND OMEGA** Revelation 1:8;22:13

**AMEN** Revelation 3:14

**ANOINTED** Acts 10:38

**ANOINTED ONE** Luke 3:21

**APOSTLE OF OUR PROFESSION** Hebrews 3:1

**ATONING SACRIFICE FOR OUR SINS** 1 John 2:2

AUTHOR OF LIFE Acts 3:15

AUTHOR AND FINISHER OF OUR FAITH Hebrews 12:2

AUTHOR OF SALVATION Hebrews 2:10

BEGINNING AND END Revelation. 22:13

BEGOTTEN SON 1 John 4:9

BELOVED SON 2 Peter 1:17

BLESSED AND ONLY RULER 1 Timothy 6:15

BLESSED OF GOD 1 Timothy 1:11

BLESSED HOPE Titus 2:13

BREAD OF GOD John 6:33

BREAD OF LIFE John 6:35; 6:48

BRIDEGROOM Matthew 9:15

BRIGHT AND MORNING STAR Revelation 22:16

CAPTAIN OF MAN'S SALVATION Hebrews 2:10

CHIEF CORNERSTONE Ephesians 2:20

CHIEF SHEPHERD 1 Peter 5:4

CHRIST 1 John 2:22

COMFORTER Lamentations 1:16

COUNSELOR Isaiah 9:6

CREATOR OF ALL THINGS John 1:3

THE ENDUEMENT OF POWER Luke 24:49

THE ETERNAL SPIRIT Hebrews 9:14

AN EXCELLENT SPIRIT Daniel 5:12

THE FINGER OF GOD Luke 11:20

FLOODS ON THE DRY GROUND Isaiah 44:3

FOUNTAIN OF WATER John 4:14

FULLNESS OF GOD Ephesians 3:19

**GENEROUS SPIRIT** Psalms 51:12

**GATEKEEPER** John 10:3

**GIFT OF GOD** John 4:10; Acts 8:20

**GIFT OF THE HOLY SPIRIT** Acts 2:38

**GLORY OF THE LORD** 2 Cor. 3:18

**GOD** Acts 5:4

**GOOD SPIRIT** Neh. 9:20

**GUARANTEE OF OUR INHERITANCE** Eph. 1:14; cf. 2 Cor. 5:5

# MODULE EIGHT

# SPIRITUAL WARFARE: IT IS TIME TO FIGHT

- The Mind
- Spiritual Warfare: What is it?
- Defensive vs. Offensive
- Know Your Enemy
- Tools of the Enemy
- The Fight is all about Identity
- Why does God allow the Enemy Power?

## PRAYER TARGET

Lord, I pray as David did: 'Teach my hands to war and my fingers to do battle'. Show me how to strategically destroy strongholds in my life for the sake of my future (**Psalm 144:1**). Jehovah Gibbor (the God who Defends/the Man of War), manifest now and train me.

## #MCBRIDEMOMENT

There is a prolific misconception regarding who humanity's enemy is. It is never the person that disagrees with our progress. Our enemy is not those we deem as haters or those festering in sullied jealousy. The undaunted enemy we all share is the kingdom of darkness, the author of spiritual wickedness in high places. I believe we master tactics of spiritual warfare when we are committed to fighting for our earthly families.

To fully understand the battle that is taking place around us, we must first acknowledge that we are at war. Although the fight is fixed in our favor because of what Jesus did for us on the cross, it still does not repudiate the fact that there is a war taking place around us daily. The battles we encounter are simply small sections to the overall bigger picture.

Conflict between two persons, factions, and armies consisting of any type of "extended contest, struggle, or controversy" is essentially what makes a battle. As people of faith, there is always some sort of spiritual mêlée taking place around us. Just as warfare are battles fought on various territories, for many reasons and with fluctuating progressions of intensity in the natural, it is essentially the same for warfare in the spirit.

Our spiritual confrontations are real, even though we cannot readily see our attacker. However, we can bring ourselves into practical awareness and understanding on how the battles are fought as well as how they impact our realities on an everyday basis. Spiritual Warfare is nothing more than our vying to have life, in our reality, identically mirror the way God wants it to be. It is a battle for our mind between our evil imaginations (influenced by satanic suggestions, life circumstances, faithlessness, etc) and the glorious knowledge of God. The overall objective of spiritual warfare, for the believer, is to "have the mind of Christ."

**Spiritual Warfare** is simply the Believer's resistance, overcoming, and defeating the enemy's lie (deception, temptations, and accusations) that he sends our way. There are two types of spiritual warfare I have come to identify, and each requires various levels of tenacity and response. They are:

- Defensive- essentially the act of defending one's territory. It is where one has been forced into battle in response to an attack from an opponent, and a defensive response exhibited to outwit an offensive act. Defensive warfare does not advance into the enemy's camp. Such defensive type of warfare is necessary because Satan is constantly attacking believers and therefore, we should be constantly alert to apply defensive strategies in order to defend our spiritual territories.

- Offensive- a hostile combat against the adversary that is depicted by its forceful nature and not passively anticipating the enemy to introduce his assault. This type of warfare aggressively goes into the enemy's territory and gaining, rather than losing, ground.

Offensive warfare is based solely on information. The enemy is recognized, as well as his tactics, and the assault engaged against him is based on the intel gained [ref. Spiritual Mapping]. In spiritual offensive warfare, the Believer assaults satan's kingdom with the intent of liberating other believers or emancipating themselves from hell's captivity (i.e., the backslider encountering an Evangelist).

## WHO IS THE ENEMY?

1. Lucifer [Ezekiel 28:12-15; Isaiah 14:12-15, **Jude 6, Luke 10:18-19**]

- **He WAS:** the personification of worship, the covering of God's very throne, the embodiment of GLORY (his worship reflected glory), the pinnacle of Influence in Heaven. He was creativity personified and encapsulated in a Being.

- **He HAD:** wisdom and authority above all others, stood in the place of ultimate influence in heaven, the epicenter of the Creator's joy. He WAS the Morning Star, the supreme servant of God

- **He IS:** the birthplace of Iniquity [**hebrew word:** avon, means crookedness, a perversity...literally means to turn in the opposite direction] He coveted the worship and honor of heaven. The moment Lucifer's priority shifted from reflecting the glory of God in worship, to seeking glory for himself, he entertained "I can be just like God" and LOST IT ALL. He was stripped of peace and cast down (Luke 10:18-19)

2. Satan

- Lucifer substituted his unending attractiveness for the skin of a serpent and slithered into the Garden of Eden. He left his God-given abode of reverence to the God of the universe and assumed an eternal residence in the accusation of humanity. As a result, his name shifted from Lucifer (Angel of Light) to Satan (Accuser) **Genesis 3:4-5 [ref. Isaiah 14:13-14]**. Satan echoed in the garden to Eve what he said to himself during his initial fall (**hebrew:** napal, means to fall, to be thrown down, to drop). He used his gift of influence to project his idea of being like God on to Eve. Humanity's nature is not iniquity...Satan's nature is! Humanity's nature is to be on the right path with God, being driven by praise. Humanity had a tempter; Lucifer did not. He chose to operate in his iniquity, and as a result he was disqualified from receiving God's redemption.

- Humanity stands in the place of intimacy that Lucifer lost, and we can ONLY shift from this place if we permit our focus to be shifted.

Lucifer NEVER lost his ability to influence or suggest. This is the crux of his weaponry to this present day. His role in Heaven was to instigate worship. At his movement the act of worship was suggested and pursued by the Beings of Heaven. Satan wants humanity to also shift our focus from God to ourselves. At his fall, Lucifer was FILLED with, "I will." The issue was never with what God willed but what he willed. Whatever serves to enrich us at the expense of God's glory is iniquity. Guard your focus by any means necessary, as it is the driving force of your sobriety. Just as the Believer has tools and weapons, so does our enemy. We must be aware of our opponent and his tactics, as well as the enablement Heaven has given us. Here is a list of some of the weapons the kingdom of darkness uses, but also the anti-tactics the Believer holds:

- **Illusion** is Hell's ultimate agenda to make the Believer think Satan has power. Satan does have power, but it is unquestionably bound by the legal systems of Heaven. He cannot use his power, authority, or will any way he would like simply because he is held in check by God who has humanity's best interest in mind. It is an age-old truth that will never change. Jesus won the victory over the kingdom of darkness, but He leaves it to humanity to superimpose that victory. Intercessor know that if the enemy is manifesting havoc in your life, you have the responsibility and power to stop as well as apprehend him.

- **Luke 10:19 (AMP)** "Listen carefully: I have given you authority [that you now possess] to tread on serpents and scorpions, and [the ability to exercise authority] over all the power of the enemy (Satan); and nothing will [in any way] harm you."

- **Matthew 28:18 (NIV)** "All authority in heaven and on earth has been given to me. Therefore, go and make disciples of all nations."

- **Deception** is the act of making someone accept a lie as if it is the truth. When Satan sends deception our way, it is an ultimate endeavor to swindle us into accepting his lie so that we will live a life consumed in inaccuracy

  - **Belt of Truth** (defensive) assists us in safeguarding people, places and things against the enemy's deception/lie (Ephesians 6:14)

  - **Sword of the Spirit** (offensive) assists us in destroying the prevailing deception that exists in the minds of humanity (Ephesians 6:17). These prevailing diabolical thoughts are nothing more than demonic strongholds and imaginations exalting themselves above the mind of Christ. Romans 12:2 suggests that we should renew our minds. HOW? By deliberately learning the Word; Ephesians 5:26 calls it washing by the water of the Word.

- **Temptation** is when we are lured or admonished to miss God in one way or another, to willingly become the antithesis of what God has commissioned us to be. Temptation comes immediately after deception has been utilized, see Genesis 3. Biblically, it is suggested that Eve believed Satan's propaganda (deception), and as a result what was forbidden was now **seemingly** satisfying and undamaging (temptation). Eventually she acted (sinned) and invited Adam to do the same. In Matthew 4, we see Jesus is tempted, however Jesus beat Satan down by utilizing the Word of God. Jesus was so saturated in the Word that he calmly resisted with no perception of duality (**Psalm 119:11,** WORD sustains us from the fall).

- **Resistance** (defensive) - actively denying the enemy access to our capacity to make decisions and produce actions whenever he attempts to make suggestions. **James 4:7 (AMP)** "So submit to [the authority of] God. Resist the devil [stand firm against him] and he will flee from you.

- **Submission/Surrender** (offensive)- the act of consenting or yielding to a greater force or to the authority or will of another person; submission is to be subject to a specific practice, action, or situation

- **Accusations** Satan is identified as one who attempts to shame a Believer based on the vileness of their past and imperfections of their present. He consistently attempts to remind us of those blemishes and wear us out with condemnation and guilt for the things we have done that are all covered by the shed blood of Jesus Christ (Ephesians 6:16). The difference between the Believer and Satan is the undaunted fact that we have a loving Redeemer that daily covers us in His righteousness.

- **Shield of Faith (defensive)** the accusations Hell employs against a person, place or thing is what Ephesians 6:16 calls fiery darts. When the kingdom of darkness attempts to accuse us of our past or current offenses, we have faith in the saving grace of the cross and the accepted illuminating knowledge of salvation, that we are forgiven. Faith is what we use to extinguish the fiery darts of the enemy (Ephesians 6:16). We are not to contemplate about our past from a place of guilt, simply because it has passed away (2 Corinthians 5:17), and our sins have been forgotten (Hebrews 10:17).

- **Breastplate of Righteousness (offensive)** "Righteous" is who and what we are, even on a bad day! The righteousness the Believer exhibits only comes from Christ. Without Christ, humanity's righteousness is as filthy rags (Isaiah 64:6), but because of Calvary and Jesus' blood we receive God's righteousness solely through Christ (Romans 3:22). Salvation and blessings are freely given to all who receive the gift of saving grace given by God. Satan constantly disputes the will of God. As a result, we have to employ our Advocate, Jesus, to defeat him in the courts of heaven. Jesus has never lost a case and seals our 'court papers' with His blood; the accusations are thrown out and the case is close!

## WHERE DOES THE BATTLE OF SPIRITUAL WARFARE TAKE PLACE ULTIMATELY?

2 Corinthians 10:3-5 (NIV) "For though we live in the world, we do not wage war as the world does. The weapons we fight with are not the weapons of the world. On the contrary, they have divine power to demolish strongholds. We demolish arguments and every pretension that sets itself up against the knowledge of God, and we take captive every thought to make it obedient to Christ."

Some translations have arguments, theories, reasonings, speculations, knowledge, and thoughts. ALL of these belong in the same realm: the MIND and ultimately the area of the soul.

**Strongholds** are thoughts [either diabolical or righteous] that have taken territory of the mind and affect the way by which we live life. In the hands of darkness, they are nothing more than incorrect thinking patterns based on lies instigated by Hell. Webster defines it as a place where a particular cause or belief is strongly defended or upheld. From belief in the lies of hell, accusations and deception gain ground in the mind and influence in behavior.

Tools used to build diabolical strongholds - **abandonment, abuse, abortion, accident, accusations, addictions, adultery, adversity, affliction, anger, anxiety, apathy, approval-seeking behavior, arguments, attachments, avoidance, backlash, backsliding, betrayal, blind spots, bitterness, compromise, CONTAMINATED ANOINTING, delusion, degenerative disease, deception, depression, discouragement, laziness, fear, false burdens, false entitlement, false expectations, false impressions. FIERY DARTS, FRIENDLY FIRE, gossip,** frustration, generational curses, guilt, insecurity, iniquity, incest, immaturity, incest, ignorance, judgmentalism, jealousy, lies, lust, manipulation, materialism, miseducation, negativity, MOVING OUT OF THE TIMING OF GOD, mistrust, rebellion, regret, rape, pride, etc. (The Rules of Engagement: the Art of Strategic Prayer and Spiritual Warfare by Cindy Trimm).

## THE FIGHT IS ALL ABOUT IDENTITY

### Where You See GOD Incorrectly

Individuals that perceive God as a tyrant will live in an unhealthy fear of God. This type of fear-based reverence robs the believer of enjoying the love and rhapsody that comes with receiving the resurrection power of God gifted through salvation. There is a noble type of fear of God that is more of a holy respect for who God is. But there is another type of fear that Satan desires humanity to exhibit. That fear is rooted in the perception that God is punishing, unsympathetic, aloof, hardhearted and would crack the whip at us the moment we deviate from His desires. Those who feel that they have fallen too far from God or have committed some inexcusable sin live under the authority of this type of stronghold. Those who feel that it is hard to sense the love and presence of God have also yielded themselves to this stronghold too. Wherever we find ourselves questioning the love of God for us, identifying Him as distant and unapproachable, we must aggressively dismantle this stronghold that has been erected in our minds.

### Where You See YOURSELF Incorrectly

Those of us who suffer from toxic self-views find it difficult to bear witness to the new person we have now become in

Christ. It is a form of low self-esteem, due to its effect to incapacitate our ability to view self as worthy of God's love. This frame of mind establishes blockades to accepting what Christ did for all of humanity and how His works apply to who we are. Usual indicators of this stronghold are: feelings of guiltiness, searching if we have genuinely been pardoned of our sins, low spiritual esteem (accepting the lie that we are sinners, not saints), the lack of spiritual fortitude that we are assumed to have in Christ Jesus, we may even appear double minded due to our internal struggles with sinfulness (Jesus said that if you stay in His Word, which tears down strongholds, you will be free from the power sin has over you - John 8:31-34), and overall there is no manifested joy in our serving the Lord. It is as if salvation, righteousness, and holiness have become a dreadful chore.

**WE TEAR DOWN STRONGHOLDS** by consuming the truth of God's Word, which is furthest from what the enemy has been serving us. The weapon we use to tear down strongholds is found in Ephesians 6:17, "...the sword of the Spirit, which is the word of God." Keep in mind, the sword is an offensive weapon utilized to demolish all forces of resistance. Strongholds are assets in wars for whichever side chooses to utilize them. Again, remember that strongholds are nothing more than perpetual thoughts by which we govern our lives. Utilize the weapon of the Word of God, the Sword of the Spirit, to carnage the enemy's assets but to also establish the Lord strongholds!

## Why Does God Allow the Devil to Have Such Power?

**Genesis 2:15-17 (AMP)** "So the Lord God took the man [He had made] and settled him in the Garden of Eden to cultivate and keep it. And the Lord God commanded the man, saying,

"You may freely (unconditionally) eat [the fruit] from every tree of the garden; but [only] from the tree of the knowledge (recognition) of good and evil you shall not eat, otherwise on the day that you eat from it, you shall most certainly die [because of your disobedience]."

Because humanity is the offspring of Adam and Eve, we also have this knowledge of Good and Evil, as well as the nature to pursue evil. Since God is good and there is no evil in Him (**James 1:13, 17 AMP**), God cannot tolerate the evil that is innately in us. Is it possible that God permits Satan to continue his existence to show humanity the difference between Good and Evil to help us make the right choice (Deuteronomy 30:15, 19)? After all, the scripture admonishes us that all things are conspiring together, working towards the common goal of good, towards us that love God. Hell is the only nemesis we have, and even with all of its craftiness it is still a victorless place. Ultimately, I believe the Kingdom of Darkness is only around to perfect us (Romans 8:18-38). Intercessor NEVER permit the instrument of fear to determine how you engage the enemy! Know that hell has a prolific hatred for you and will do anything and everything necessary to cause you to forfeit your God-given life. Find rest in the victory Jesus has given, knowing that it is insurmountable. Find strength to daily legislate that victory. Find hunger to prudently study the Word of God, so you will always know what God has deemed permissible.

### REMEMBER!

- Satan is NOT all powerful. All power and dominion belong to God and God alone (Jude 1:25, Psalm 62:11, Matthew 6:13)
- Although Satan is not powerful, he can still influence

humanity so that our lives are marked by disobedience and rebellion towards God, which are doors Hell uses to enlarge its territory [Isaiah 5:12-15, hell enlarges itself off humanity's ignorance and disregard for who God is].

# CELEBRATION ASSIGNMENT

### "Will you FIGHT for YOU?"

Identify the demonically-influenced strongholds in your life, document the history of these strongholds (track them as far as you can). This would essentially look like a genogram, documenting the lives and toxic behaviors of your ancestors. Find scripture that counters them.

EX. *Stronghold of low self-esteem and self-value, came from my maternal and paternal grandmothers who accepted physical and verbal abuse for decades.*

**SCRIPTURE:** Psalm 139:14 "I will give thanks to You, for I am fearfully and wonderfully made; Wonderful are Your works, And my soul knows it very well."

For the next seven days, FIGHT against that which is FIGHTING YOU (this is Offensive and Defensive Warfare)! Utilize the tools and weapons identified in Modules 6 & 7. You have the right to fight from the place of the identity God has given you! ARISE.

# NOTES

_____

_____

_____

_____

_____

_____

_____

_____

_____

_____

_____

_____

_____

_____

_____

_____

_____

_____

_____

_____

_____

_____

_____

_____

_____

# APPENDIX

# THE CHARGE

Charges have been used throughout history to remind humanity of its responsibility to authority, power, and community. The purpose of this book is to remind readers daily communication with God is urgently important, but to also active hearts to pray. I have called on a few of my Friends to release charges over us, as we pursue God in faith. Thank you for purchasing The Pursuit and journey with me.

-McBride

# THE CHARGE: FOR THE MAN

*But for now, I feel a stirring in my heart to send Epaphroditus*
*back to you immediately. He's a friend to me and a wonderful*
*brother, and fellow soldier who has worked with me as we*
*serve as ministers of the gospel. It's true he almost died but*
*God showed him mercy and healed him. And I'm so thank-*
*ful to God for his healing, as I was spared from having the*
*sorrow...*

**Philippians 2:25, 27 (TPT)**

My Brother, in this most profound, powerful and poignant moment rife with the possibilities only known to the supernatural, I, like Paul the Apostle am stirred to release the ancient mantle of prayer and intercession not only into your life but your loins. May the priestly anointing of Christ – our Chief Intercessor – quicken you and reverberate through your lineage, invoking the "last day anointing."

As you have journeyed through this book you have uncovered incredible mysteries to which your sons and daughters will prophesy. This moment transcends time and trends excavating treasures within your earthen vessel guaranteeing a consistent trajectory of triumph. I release upon you the anointing of Epaphroditus (Philippians 2:25-30, Philippians 4:18) may you survive, thrive and be found releasing strength wherever your journey takes you.

According to Proverbs 17:17, as Friend you are always loyal and as a Brother you are born for adversity. Fellow Soldier, according to 1 Timothy 6:11-12, I charge you to pursue righteousness, godliness, faith, love, endurance and gentleness. Fight the good fight of faith." Like Epaphroditus, this last season almost killed you, but the mercy of God prevailed and healed you.

**His mercy heals your mind.**
**His mercy heals your will.**
**His mercy heals your emotions.**
**His mercy heals your spirit.**
**His mercy heals your perspective.**
**His mercy heals your resolve.**
**His mercy heals your fight.**
**His mercy heals your manhood.**

I, like Paul, thank God for your healing. I call you Epaphroditus. Because of God's mercy and your healing, nations and generations of Men will be spared the sorrow of trauma, confusion, anxiety, failed potential, broken dreams, shattered hopes and premature death.

**Because YOU have healed and healed well:**

**I charge you to walk in the anointing of Jairus.**
*You stand between certain death and our daughters. "Do not*

*be afraid; just believe, and she will be healed."*
*(Luke 8:50 NIV)*

I charge you to walk in the anointing of the Centurion.
*You are a man under authority. When you speak, the plague of physical, emotional, mental, emotional, spiritual, systemic, structural and cyclical paralysis must cease.*
*(Matthew 8:8 NIV)*

I charge you to walk in the anointing of the Certain Man.
*In your kneel, hell unnerves. In your cry, the power of darkness cry. As you access the mercy of God, our sons will be loosed from every diabolical assault on their destiny, direction and dreams. (Matthew 17:1-21)*

I charge you to walk in the anointing of Simeon.
*Because of the weight and wait of your intercession in this hour, you will not taste death until you see what you have seen. (Luke 2:27)*

I charge you to pursue nations and kingdoms. Uproot and tear down, destroy and overthrow, build and plant in intercession! GO!

Lawrence A. Beasley
Chicago, IL

# THE CHARGE: FOR THE WOMAN

Prayer is perhaps one of the most misunderstood, mishandled and underemployed technologies that heaven has made available to the believer. I've personally seen first hand the functionality of intercession completely transform the lives of countless individuals. Conversely, I've also witnessed how lives, relationships and purposes have fallen prey to the subterfuge of the enemy. This has become reality because somewhere we have failed to understand the power and practicality of prayer. Honestly, my very existence is a walking billboard that attests to the fact that prayer has the ability to cause the broken pieces of your life to come together to become a breathtakingly radiant edifice that heralds the goodness of the Father.

For years, it appears that prayer has been shrouded in layers of lofty theological supposition and frankly deemed as "a woman's work". If we're very transparent, that ideology alone has bullied many of us out of a posture that has the ability to rewrite history. The very first present truth that my Grandmother and Mother instilled in me regarding their legacy of prayer is that it is an honor to call upon the name of the Lord and wait on Him. They trained me to understand that as a woman, waiting upon the Lord has a value that far exceeds the rarest jewel and power that can't be matched.

There are various examples within the sacred text that discloses how worlds were changed because a woman decided to lay down her life in the place of prayer and intercession. It was the prayers of a woman by the name of Prophetess Anna who divulged mysteries and proclaimed the coming of Christ in the temple. It was the prayers of a woman by the name of Esther who utilized wisdom to entreat the heart of a king and ultimately save her bloodline. Today, it will be the prayers of a woman who has diligently traveled through the previous pages of this manual who will posture herself to receive the charge to change the trajectory of outcomes and even her own bloodline. *Sisters, it's you.*

The essence of femininity is receiving. Therefore, the very inability to exercise vulnerability and a willingness to receive is a direct assault from hell on womanhood. Woman's DNA was molded in the hands of God to enable us to acquire and incubate. However, hard heartedness poisons and stagnates daughters. If assiduously applied, these pages have the ability to equip you to wage war and prevail against any assault that would attempt to barricade you out of your God-given privilege to carry heavy matters in the place of prayer. Unprocessed pain will disciple us into levels of hardness that will ultimately rob us of reproducing.

The enemy of our souls is banking on us being aloof, overextended with life and family, wounded and isolated. He wants us to continue to make the decision to drop the ball. He craves for us to despise our womanhood. But sisters — *not you.*

May the pages that you've journeyed through in this manual galvanize you and ultimately catapult you into your divine designation to carry. Weep. Nurture. Dream. Instruct. Innovate. Bridge. Love. All to the glory of God.

Sisters –– May you ascend. May you arise and legislate. May you live without shame of the past. May you pray without fear of the future. Long live the daughters. PRAY, GIRL!

Sharde D. Martin
Atlanta, GA

# THE CHARGE: FOR THE CHILD

Oftentimes children are overlooked because of our ages and the perception that kids are not wise. However, God speaks to us clearly because we have no alternative, selfish motive other than to see God for ourselves. So today I charge you to never lose your purity of heart and pursuit of God. May God grant you language for where you are now, and light for where He is going to take you. May the children ARISE and cause the Earth to shake with revival or revolution! May the children ARISE and be authentic carriers of God's glory, power, answers, solutions and demonstration! May the children ARISE and pray God sized prayers that loose God sized answers in everything we pray/intercede about. Families, Communities, Churches, States, Nations will all turn to God when the Children pray.

Dear God,

Thank you for the opportunities You have given us as sons and daughters, to carry a torch for your kingdom. Just as You called Jeremiah at a young age, we believe that You are now doing the same for us. We understand that You desire for us to not only to live life, but to live on fire for You and fully focused on the calling placed on our lives. We thank You for the tender mercies You have shown us each and every day, though we continue to sin against You. We ask that You forgive us for any and all sins of disobedience, and we thank You for being amazing and gracious to us.

Lord, we give our lives to You. All that we are, and all that we have is Yours. We surrender to Your Will. We pray that You would have Your way with, in and through us. Holy Spirit, we ask that You begin to quicken in us. Father, we ask that Your fire would begin to stir in us. We pray that You would begin to burn everything in us that is not like You, and that You would let the gifts You placed inside us begin to awaken. **2 Timothy 1:6** tells us to stir the gift You have given us. Let Your power fall upon us right now, and Your Word be accomplished through us. Father use us! That is our hearts cry, USE US!

We are Your servants, and we wait on Your command. We pray that Your fire would blow through our veins, and revive our spiritual DNA, setting this next generation ablaze for You. We welcome You into our lives and ask that You transform us. This place where we stand is Yours, and You are welcome.

Make our hearts pure, and our motives Your motives. We bind and cast out anxiety, fear, and depression, we pray that the assignment of Hell would not follow through in our lives. For You have not given us a spirit of fear, but of power, love, and a sound mind (**2 Timothy 1:7**). And because of this, we can move forward in the power of the Holy Spirit through prayer, performing miracles, signs, and wonders! We pray Your grace and mercy would continue to follow us wherever our feet may tread, in Jesus Name, Amen.

Micaiah Wilson,
Atlanta, GA

# AUTHOR ACKNOWLEDGEMENTS

To my maternal Grandparents and Mother: Albert McBride Sr., Golena McBride & Sandra McBride-Jordan, you all taught me the power of prayer and introduced me to the God of answers. I am because of who you all submitted yourselves...to the True and Living God.

To my Mentor and Safe-Space: Dorretta Adams you taught me how to believe God for others and pray bold prayers. Your fearlessness and leadership safeguarded my life throughout my undergraduate years. Although you are no longer physically with us, this book exists because of your pour. God is answering your prayers! I love and miss you dearly 'Ma Adams'.

To my Framily Group: Sharde Martin, Tonthalell Walters, Samuel and Ayanna Giles, Christopher and Gale Jones, Isaiah and Brandi Robertson III, Dion and Jennifer Leonard, Claude Hamilton, Cheneka Hobbs, Ernest and Latia Vaughan, Kenneth and Raven Nole, Lawrence and Quentesa Beasley, Karlene and Mikke Hamilton, Carl and Hope McKinnon, Phillip and Je'neen Small, Christopher Percy, Byanka Tucker and Lauren Aqeel you all have impacted my life in ways that are indescribable. Your journey's, faith and love kept me anchored when I wanted to give up. Your Friendship has authentically watered my soul in some of the weariest seasons. Thank you! Your proximity to my life taught me that proper community is an instrument of the Lord's protection. Your prayers, friendship and love have saved my life.

To my Godchildren: Carlie Faith McKinnon and Phillip Small, Jr whenever I see you...I see the fruit of what prayer and faith can do. I pray that my ceiling is your floor, may you both change the World for the better. I love you!

To my Pastors: LaBryant and Phineka Friend, you both have simultaneously been an oasis of healing for me. In 2017 you both gave me space into your ministry and also your lives. Who could have known those selfless acts would incubate and birth *The Pursuit?*

To my Wife: Channing B. McBride, you are my heart...my Person. Experiencing your love has pushed me deeper to God. THANK YOU! I look forward to watching God move through our marriage and sharing as colaborers with His will in the Earth. I love you, deeply.

# MEET THE
# AUTHOR

Broderick L. McBride is a thought leader and master communicator. He fully embraces the notion that mental health and spirituality go hand-in-hand, an idea that is deeply engrafted in his teaching and counseling style.

Quickly rising as an influential voice in various sectors and communities, McBride travels locally and nationally as a lecturer, facilitator, public theologian, and mission-based activist. Dubbed as an Intergenerational Griot, he is fond of creating spaces that bridges generational gaps and assisting with exposing lived narratives amongst the generations. Merging his faith praxis and interest for social justice, he has become well known for his meaningful contributions to conversations that aid in the reforming of cultures.

The mid-South native is both a master storyteller and demonstrative speaker. His out-of-the-box style of bringing life to the word of God has permitted him to travel nationally and internationally. McBride is a mental health advocate, with a social justice edge. He is slated to release a variety of tools and publications centered on his most notable lectures and research.

He is an alumnus of Morehouse College and Emory University.

A family man above all, he is happily married to Channing B. McBride, and together they reside in the metro Atlanta area.

# CONNECT WITH THE AUTHOR

Thank you for reading, *The Pursuit*. Broderick looks forward to connecting with you. Here are a few ways you can connect with the author and stay updated on new releases, speaking engagements, products, and more.

**FACEBOOK**      Broderick L. McBride

**INSTAGRAM**      @broderick.mcbride

**WEBSITE**      www.broderickmcbride.com

**PODCAST**      *The Let Outt Podcast* Available on Apple Podcasts, Spotify, Google Play, Google Podcasts, and Anchor

Made in the USA
Columbia, SC
10 February 2021

32173869R00093